A voyage of discovery

A voyage
of discovery

The ups and downs
of the Christian life

Derek Thomas

EP BOOKS
Faverdale North, Darlington, DL3 0PH, England

e-mail: sales@epbooks.org
web: http://www.epbooks.org

EP BOOKS USA
P. O. Box 614, Carlisle, PA 17013, USA

e-mail: usasales@epbooks.org
web: http://www.epbooks.us

First published 2001
This edition 2011

British Library Cataloguing in Publication Data available

ISBN-13: 978-0-85234-742-3   ISBN-10: 0-85234-742-1

Unless otherwise indicated, all Scripture quotations are from The Holy Bible, English Standard Version, published by HarperCollins Publishers © 2001 by Crossway Bibles, a division of Good News Publishers. Used by permission. All rights reserved.

Printed and bound in Italy by   Grafica Veneta.

To

Ligon and Anne Duncan

With gratitude for the last decade of ministry together

Acknowledgements

'Be thankful,' Paul urges us (Col. 3:15), and it is proper that a word or two acknowledging the help of others be given here. No book is without its first-draft errors of grammar and style (at least, no book of *mine*, that is!), and I am grateful to the sharp eyes of my Thornwell Scholar, Marshall Brown, and my secretary, Ruth Bennett, for their cheerful labours on my behalf. Mention must be made of those who employ these fine folk (and myself!): Reformed Theological Seminary. I am deeply thankful for the friendship offered by my colleagues and the support of the administration at the seminary that provide the time and incentive for writing.

EP Books have published a number of my books and I am grateful to them for their enthusiasm with this offering. In particular, I wish to thank Sue Holmes for her wonderful skills as an editor.

I have only come to know Don Whitney personally in recent years, but we share a common burden for 'spiritual formation'. Given his well-known expertise in this area, his kind words of endorsement on the cover of this volume lend me encouragement that I am on the right track. Sinclair Ferguson has been a friend and mentor of mine for over thirty years, and his willingness to associate with these words of mine is humbling and deeply appreciated. Dr Ferguson's ministry on both sides of the Atlantic is justly praised, and I count it a singular honour that he agreed to write the foreword.

What would I be without my family? To my wife, Rosemary, and to my two children, Ellen and Owen, I offer an extended 'hug' of gratitude and love. Next to my sweet Lord, you are the lights of my life.

These pages were originally delivered in the form of sermons at the mid-week prayer and Bible-study hour at First Presbyterian Church, Jackson, Mississippi, where I now serve as Minister of Teaching. To the longsuffering folk of 'First Pres' I am deeply grateful, not least to the senior minister, Dr Ligon Duncan. Ligon is both my boss and a personal friend, and serving with him at this fine, historic church has been the greatest honour of my life. It is to Ligon and his dear wife, Anne, that I dedicate this book.

Contents

Foreword

S ome time ago I met an acquaintance whom I had not seen for several weeks. It was immediately obvious that he had lost weight and was looking in very much better shape. When I commented on this he replied enthusiastically, 'Yes, I have been on a diet designed by the Mayo Clinic.' As the conversation continued, it emerged that the diet covered a two-week period and provided a disciplined foundation for him to be in better health for the future. That, of course, is (or ought to be) the point of a diet: to provide a basic restructuring of habits which, if continued, will improve health, well-being and our overall performance. In this instance, apparently, it had been very successful — as one would expect from a diet carefully researched and field-tested by an internationally-renowned hospital.

Here, Derek Thomas provides us with the spiritual equivalent of the Mayo Clinic Diet. In these pages you will find a carefully researched two-week programme designed to help you reshape and re-discipline a daily time of Bible study, meditation and prayer.

We tend to trust such programmes as the Mayo Clinic Diet, because we know they have been designed by reliable

clinicians and have been well tested. The same is true here.
Derek Thomas is a reliable, widely respected, long-experienced
student of Scripture and the spiritual life, a pastor of Christ's
sheep, a scholar, a theologian and a teacher of theological
students. So here is a clinician of the soul who can be trusted
to give reliable guidance and solid biblical wisdom.

But, more than that, the basic programme which Dr Thomas
here prescribes for us — the Songs of Ascent, Psalms 120 –
134 — has had the most rigorous field testing. He has tested it
himself. In addition, it has been given the most rigorous use by
countless numbers of believers spreading over three millennia.

Above all, this programme was field-tested by the 'founder
… of our faith' (Heb. 12:2), Jesus himself. From the time
he was twelve years old he must have sung them, either *en
route* to Jerusalem, or during the days he was there, asking
questions in the temple, amazing the Jewish scholars with his
knowledge of the Lord and his Word. The way in which Dr
Luke records that event seems to me to reflect the wonderful
words of Psalm 27:4 and 8 (NIV):

> One thing I ask of the LORD,
>   this is what I seek:
> that I may dwell in the house of the LORD
>   all the days of my life,
> to gaze upon the beauty of the LORD
>   and to seek him in his temple…
> My heart says of you, 'Seek his face!'
>   Your face, LORD, I will seek.

Here, then, is an invitation to spend two weeks in a spiritual exercise which has brought countless blessings to God's
people in every age — and one which our Lord Jesus himself
field-tested and found to be wholly reliable. Like the Mayo

Clinic Diet, it requires commitment; it involves discipline; there may even be some pain. But of this you can be sure, if I may paraphrase the apostle Paul a little: while the appetite, discipline and training of the Mayo Clinic Diet is of some value, this spiritual training will help to reshape your whole life and bring rich and lasting benefits.

Sinclair B. Ferguson
Glasgow
July 2001

Preface

The folks at EP Books have kindly asked me to 'revise' this book, previously titled *Making the Most of Your Devotional Life*, and first published almost a decade ago. I have gladly agreed, partly because I continue to appreciate these psalms (Psalms of Ascent) as expressive of much of what makes up our pilgrim journey, and partly because it provides me with an opportunity to freshen it up a little. To begin with, I have changed the Bible version in this edition to the English Standard Version (ESV) as representative of the best of contemporary scholarship and faithfulness to the text of Scripture. Here and there I have altered the text — shortening some sentences in light of current trends toward punchier prose, and rewriting some sections that now appear less clear than they did a decade ago.

Since writing these chapters, Alec Motyer — one of the very finest Old Testament scholars in the world today — has published his own commentary on these psalms, *Journey: Psalms for Pilgrim People*.[1] The idea of a journey is, of course, suggested by the theory that these Psalms of Ascent were gathered together to provide material reflecting the journey (pilgrimage) made by the people of God 'up' to Jerusalem in order to keep the Feasts of the Lord. The 'journey' as representative of the Christian life is apposite — think, for example, of how Christians in the early church were referred to as followers of 'the Way' (Acts 19:9; 19:23; 22:4; 24:14; 24:22); or, Bunyan's classic treatment of the Christian life, *Pilgrim's Progress*. For that reason, I gave this updated edition a new title: *A voyage of discovery — the ups and downs of the Christian life*. In the Psalms of Ascent, we discover both the depths and heights of God's ways with us — from the 'distress' of the opening psalm (Ps. 120:1), to the Lord blessing his people in the final psalm (Ps. 134:3). The Christian life is like that — it has its ups and downs, its moments of bitterness and joy, sadness and elation.

The original edition of this book was dedicated to Ligon and Anne Duncan. A decade later, I continue to be blessed by working alongside Ligon at First Presbyterian Church. I cannot begin to spell out what this means in terms of blessings for me. Suffice it to say that it has been the most privileged episode of my life — an adventure; no, a rollercoaster! I dedicate this latest edition to them with heartfelt gratitude.

Derek W. H. Thomas
Jackson, MS
March 2011

Introduction

Spirituality has become popular of late, and not just in Christian circles. From *Star Trek* to prime-time soaps, spirituality is no longer a turn-off. In this post-modern age, no one is threatened by anyone else's personal religion.

Is the modern appreciation for spirituality something to be welcomed? Is it a sign that our age is, after all, deeply religious and turning back to God? Religious it is, as every age has been (whether it has realized it or not). But it is often an expression of man's idolatry as much as anything else. Abraham Kuyper, in the *Stone Lectures* delivered at Princeton in 1898, was right when he suggested that the fundamental contrast has always been, still is, and will be to the end: Christianity or paganism, idols or the living God.

Spirituality, like everything else, needs to be evaluated in the light of the Scriptures, what God has written. Spirituality that is not in accord with the Bible is merely an expression which reveals that the human heart is lost and needs to find wholeness in biblical salvation. To cite the oft-quoted words of Augustine: 'Thou hast formed us for thyself, and our hearts are restless till they find rest in thee.'[1]

This book is designed to portray biblical spirituality as believers in the God of the Bible express it. It takes a collection of fifteen psalms, conveniently lumped together in the Hebrew canon. The collection of Psalms 120 - 134 all bear the same title: A Song of Ascents. Several theories have been put forward to explain this. Some have noticed that there are poetic features within these psalms which function almost like 'steps', rising from one thought to another. Another view notes that the word 'ascent' is related to the Hebrew verb 'to go up', which is used in Ezra 2:1, for example, of the exiles *going up* to Jerusalem. This has led to the idea that these psalms were sung by the Jewish exiles returning from Babylon to their homeland. Three of these psalms are ascribed to David (122, 124, 133), one to Solomon (127), but the rest bear no ascriptions of an author and may date from much later times in the history of the Old Testament.

A more general view is that these were sung, not by exiles, but by the Jewish diaspora as they made their way to Jerusalem in order to attend the various obligatory festivals, such as Passover (March/April), Pentecost (May/June), or the Day of Atonement (September/October). Hundreds, possibly thousands, would travel together to Jerusalem for these occasions, the procession growing as they journeyed through various towns and villages before arriving in the city itself. It is interesting to think that as they made this journey, they sang these psalms, providing food for meditation as they went. Before the Psalter was compiled in the way we have it now, this collection of psalms might have existed as a special 'hymn book' designed for a 'special occasion'.

Another view suggests that these psalms may have been sung in turn on the fifteen steps which led from one court of the temple to another (the word 'ascent' is used of 'steps' or 'stairs' in Exod. 20:26 and 1 Kings 10:19; compare Neh. 3:15;

12:37). It is suggested that the 'ascent' is to be understood in a spiritual way; these psalms are meant to convey a fifteen-step programme of meditative, spiritual progress from one degree to another. Some movement is readily discernible in them, and they can function very easily as guides to growth and maturity in the faith. The 'spiritual person' (1 Cor. 2:15), as Paul refers to him, needs to be fed spiritually. These psalms do just that.

Christian tradition offers many examples of similar attempts to recharge batteries when energy output threatens to come to an end. From such writings as Augustine's *Confessions*, Anselm of Canterbury's *Monologion*, Ignatius Loyola's *Spiritual Exercises*, or the principal writings of the Carthusian prior, Guigo II, *Scalaclaustralium*,[2] works abound offering spiritual rejuvenation through an intense reflection on Christian doctrine and/or experience. In our own time, James I. Packer's *Knowing God*, though not written with this purpose in mind, has, nevertheless, been used in precisely this way to considerable advantage.

Loyola is an interesting example. He is, possibly, one of the most important of the spiritual writers of the sixteenth century. Born *c.*1491 in Spain, he served briefly in the army of the Duke of Nájera, only to suffer a leg wound which forced him into a prolonged period of convalescence in the castle at Loyola. There he read Ludolf of Saxony's *Life of Christ* which projects the reader, imaginatively, into the life of Jesus of Nazareth. The book caused Loyola to desire a reformation in his own life. His course of reform involved a pilgrimage to Jerusalem. During this journey, Loyola wrote the *Spiritual Exercises* in which he suggests a course of four weeks in which the reader studies and meditates on such doctrines as sin, the life of Christ, the death of Christ, and the resurrection.

If there is one consideration more humbling than another
to a spiritually-minded believer, it is, that, after all God has
done for him — after all the rich displays of his grace, the
patience and tenderness of his instructions, the repeated
discipline of his covenant, the tokens of love received, and
the lessons of experience learned, there should still exist
in the heart a principle, the tendency of which is to secret,
perpetual, and alarming departure from God.

Octavius Winslow
Personal Declension and Revival of Religion in the Soul[3]

Books such as Loyola's *Spiritual Exercises* often contain
elements which are objectionable. Similar works designed to
engage backslidden Christians into 'the deeper life' contain
doctrine that is insufficiently orthodox and clear; sometimes
the meditations are mystical in the sense of being esoteric and
experience-seeking at the expense of truth. That such works
have been written throughout church history, witness to the
fact that a structured course of self-evaluation and spiritual
reflection has proved beneficial in restoring closer communion
with God.

Consider, for example, Christian hymns. Many Christians
have found that meditating on well-known hymns has a peculiar and distinct advantage for the spiritual life. Many hymns
(and psalms, too!) deal particularly with what Richard Baxter
called 'the diseases and distempers of the soul'. They are especially useful in addressing the causes of spiritual declension.

The Psalms of Ascent function in much the same way.
Whether the various theories about their compilation have
any truth, they do appear to possess a particular quality about
them which urges the reader forward and upward, from the
doldrums of Meshech (Ps. 120:5) to the beauty and heights
of worship in Jerusalem (Ps. 122:2) and to the enjoyment of

the presence of God (Ps. 134). Along the way, we find them contemplating the dangers as they ascend towards the hills of Zion (Ps. 121). Later, upon beholding the beauty of Jerusalem, the writer of Psalm 125 bursts into a song of assurance:

> Those who trust in the LORD are like Mount Zion,
>> which cannot be moved, but abides for ever
>>> (Ps. 125:1).

The next psalm in the series finds him recalling the power demonstrated in the release they had known from captivity:

> Restore our fortunes, O LORD,
>> like streams in the Negeb!
> Those who sow in tears
>> shall reap with shouts of joy!
>>> (Ps. 126:4-5).

Just as there is geographical progress discernible, so there are valuable lessons to learn — lessons about suffering and its place within the pilgrimage that leads to the eternal city:

> 'The ploughers ploughed upon my back;
>> they made long their furrows'
>>> (Ps. 129:3).

The suffering goes even deeper:

> Out of the depths I cry to you, O LORD!
>> O Lord, hear my voice!
> Let your ears be attentive
>> to the voice of my pleas for mercy!
>>> (Ps. 130:1-2).

Learning this lesson comes closest to what Paul meant when he wrote that 'we share abundantly in Christ's sufferings' (2 Cor. 1:5). Participating in these sufferings (1 Peter 4:13) is at the heart of our pilgrimage to heaven. Calvin wrote by way of commentary on a similar passage in 1 Peter, 'The church of Christ has been from the beginning so constituted, that the cross has been the way to victory, and death a passage to life.'[4] The secret to be learned is to 'wait for the LORD' (Ps. 130:5).

One of my aims in writing this book is to provide Christians with a distinctively Reformed guide to spirituality, a book that distinguishes spirituality from mysticism on the one hand, and ambiguous and eclectic theologies on the other. The church not only needs a renewal of spirituality, but of Reformed and biblical spirituality. But what is this? Can we identify Reformed spirituality as something distinct from spirituality in general? Yes, we can! For one thing, those features that identify and distinguish the Reformed faith generally are equally valid as identifiers in the realm of piety and devotion. What are they? They are many, but five in particular shape the essential character of biblical spirituality.

Firstly, spirituality must be thoroughly theocentric. If God — that is to say, God as he reveals himself in the Bible — isn't at the heart of our spirituality, then we have something that is a hybrid. What this means in effect is this: we must think of ourselves as naturally corrupt, without interest in those things which are true, and given to that which perverts and obscures the true God. Man's mind is a perpetual factory of idols, Calvin surmised, and he was right.[5] We are by nature totally depraved, so aligned to sinful ways that only a sovereign rebirth 'from above' — to cite Jesus' words to Nicodemus (John 3:31) — can set us moving in a different direction. What we need is to be made 'a new creation' (2 Cor. 5:17), raised from spiritual death to spiritual life and resurrection, in union with Jesus

Christ (Rom. 6:4-11; Eph. 2:1-10). This frees us from our past so that what we are now 'in Christ' is radically different from what we were before 'in Adam'. This sovereign work of God in conversion forms the first and essential plank in what we may call a Reformed view of spirituality.

To be theocentric necessitates being Trinitarian. God is three persons and God is one Lord. Keeping this 'threeness in one' before us will keep us at the centre of God's revelation of himself. The Trinity is not some device conjured up by the church at Constantinople in order to baffle the minds of everyone thereafter! It is, in fact, the careful pronouncement of the church's findings as it examines the multilayered witness of Scripture to the being of God. To cite Hilary of Poitiers of the fourth century: 'God alone is fit witness of himself', and in this case, his witness is of three persons in one God. We will need the testimony of Scripture to all three persons, Father, Son and Holy Spirit, in order to achieve a well-grounded spirituality. At the same time any deviation into polytheism will damn us.

Secondly, spirituality must be Bible based and Bible driven. *Sola Scriptura*, one of the watchwords of the Reformation, will insist that in spirituality, as in everything else, the Bible must define and control. God makes his will known to us *through his Word read, explained and understood*. Paul could say of the God-breathed Scriptures, that they are 'profitable for teaching, for reproof, for correction, and for training in righteousness, that the man of God may be competent, equipped for every good work' (2 Tim. 3:16-17). One such 'good work' is the cultivation of spiritual life and vitality, and here the Scriptures must inform, motivate, encourage and shape. That will mean, at the most basic level, that Christians who desire spiritual renewal must, to cite Cranmer, 'read, mark, learn and inwardly digest' what the Bible has to say.

The 'Quiet Time' can easily degenerate into something individualistic and subjective, ignoring other dimensions of corporate life and responsibility. Reading the Psalms of Ascent, with their pervasive sense of community life, will go a long way in correcting this. But, as is so often the case, the fact that an aberration exists does not mean the thing is wrong in itself. We do need to spend time alone with God and his Word. A spirituality that fails to put the Bible (i.e. Bible reading and Bible study) at the very centre fails to appreciate *how* God speaks to us. Growth in grace can never be achieved without a serious grappling with the Scriptures and experiencing the pain of their correcting and modifying effect upon the totality of our lives.

Thirdly, spirituality must be biblically realistic — realistic, that is, about what can and cannot be achieved in this world as far as our conformity to Christ and his image is concerned; what we generally refer to as sanctification. Realistic? Yes, because unreality abounds in this area. Recognition that we live in a battlefield, surrounded within and without by implacable enemies bent on our destruction, is vital to our worldview as Christians.

The latter part of Romans 7 is vital here. We are to see ourselves as engaged in a war where total victory cannot be achieved until we get to glory. Truthfulness forces us to acknowledge that, as well as making progress, we often lose ground, too: the struggle against the world outside, the flesh within, and against the devil who manipulates both of these to curtail our progress. Thoughts of having 'arrived' will be seen as just plain zany. Important, too, will be a realism of what, or *who*, we are — that Romans 7 follows Romans 6! That means understanding that we are dead to sin and alive in Christ; that we have been buried and raised to new life in Christ.

Just as progress will be hampered, progress will also be encouraged by recalling that we are 'in Christ' in the sense that we have been raised from the dead, spiritually, into union with the risen and ascended Lord Jesus himself. This truth will give us a platform on which to make advances that nothing else will. It is the realization that we ought to make progress in sanctification because now we *can* do so. We are not 'in Adam', hampered by spiritual inability; we are 'in Christ' empowered by the Holy Spirit. This is the inexorable logic of Romans 8:10-14, where Paul reasons that, (a) we are in Christ (or, that Christ is in us); (b) we are indwelt by the same Spirit that indwelt Christ; and (c) that we have an obligation to mortify sin and put on the graces that mirror Jesus-likeness. This will keep us from an antinomian, lazy view of sanctification on the one hand, and a psychologically paralysing view of un-attainable righteousness on the other.

Fourthly, spirituality must be twin-focused — that is, both on this world and the world which is to come. It should be twin-focused because of the danger of a pietism that misses or denies the importance of life lived in *this* world, and because of an equally important danger of missing the focus of all of living here — as preparation for the world to come. Reformed spirituality will be concerned to prepare souls to live useful and productive lives in this world, appreciating all that God gives in common with everyone else living on earth.

Appreciating the creative and sustaining hand of God in all things, 'Every good gift and every perfect gift is from above, coming down from the Father' (James 1:17), will ensure that we don't miss our vocation to be 'salt' and 'light' in *this* world (Matt. 5:13-14). Equally, remembering that in this world 'we have no lasting city, but we seek the city that is to come' (Heb. 13:14), is the key note focus of New Testament Christianity.

This is not, as is so often irritatingly labelled, pietistic — as though 'to live', as Thomas Ken put it, 'each day as though thy last' was somehow misguided. This is, rather, how it ought to be. We are to live, as one puritan Chancellor told his terrified student, as those 'ready to die'. A spirituality that does not prepare us for heaven isn't worth anything.

Fifthly, spirituality must involve effort on our part as well as empowering on God's part. The relationship between sovereignty and responsibility within Reformed expressions of Christianity have sometimes been troublesome; one or other has been emphasized at the expense of, or in denial of, the other. Making too little of the necessity of effort on our side leads to passivity. Views of sanctification and growth in grace that are achieved by osmosis rather than endeavour are the result. There are views of meditation currently in vogue which come close to this view.

Reformed spirituality will not hesitate to apply Calvin's third use of the law: that we are to be motivated and impelled to seek after God with all our hearts, minds and strength, because God says so. We are culpable if we do not. Equally, we are in need of the empowering of the Holy Spirit to do so. And here, spirituality will take into consideration the various possible conditions of the soul in relationship with God. Some are healthy and others are backslidden — to cite a favourite expression of Jeremiah's (Jer. 2:19; 3:22; 4:7; 5:6; 15:6, NIV). In each (and everything in between on the spectrum of spiritual diagnosis), the Holy Spirit must come and enable us to do those things which foster and deepen our relationship with God. '... if by the Spirit you put to death the deeds of the body, you will live' (Rom. 8:13). It is we who must mortify sin and not God; but, at the same time, it is 'by the Spirit'. Calling upon God to help us in no way lessens our responsibility; but, it does keep us from a legalism that boasts self-achievement on the one hand, and a fractured mind that is frustrated by the impossible on the other.

These Psalms of Ascent continue to provide spiritual instruction to weary travellers. Their lessons have a timeless quality about them. Twenty years ago, Eugene Peterson wrote a volume on these psalms which he entitled, *A Long Obedience in the Same Direction.*[6] I have tried in this volume to approach the psalms from a different point of view, though the overall intent of both is the same: to promote a biblical view of discipleship. As we examine these psalms one by one, their cumulative force is life-changing and reforming. They point us away from introspection and self-centredness to the God of Zion whose glory ought to consume our vision.

Keeping your eye on the ball is an essential lesson in playing golf. Failure here brings tragic and embarrassing results. Equally, keeping our eye on the Lord and his glory is the lesson of these psalms (see Heb. 12:2). Taking a psalm a day, they provide us with just over two weeks in which to get in shape.

Two weeks! From the darkness of 'Kedar' in the opening psalm (120:5; *Kedar* means 'black'), we are led to an altogether different night of temple worship in the final psalm (134:1).

Two weeks! This is a goal worth pursuing.

Each day, we will spend time in one of these psalms. Read the psalm, pray over it, make notes from what you think God might be teaching you. As you read the chapter for that day, keep a journal. Donald Whitney has written:

A journal is one of the best places for charting your progress in the Spiritual Disciplines and for holding yourself accountable to your goals...[7]

At the end of each chapter I have included some questions to 'stir the juices', as it were. There are no strict rules, except the need for honesty. Writing down how we respond to God's teaching can stir the affections in a way that nothing else can.

So, there is the outline of my challenge to you.

Will *you* pursue it with me?

Psalm 120

A Song of Ascents

1 *In my distress I called to the LORD,*
    and he answered me.
2 *Deliver me, O LORD,*
    from lying lips,
    from a deceitful tongue.

3 *What shall be given to you,*
    and what more shall be done to you,
    you deceitful tongue?
4 *A warrior's sharp arrows,*
    with glowing coals of the broom tree!

5 *Woe to me, that I sojourn in Meshech,*
    that I dwell among the tents of Kedar!
6 *Too long have I had my dwelling*
    among those who hate peace.
7 *I am for peace,*
    but when I speak, they are for war!

Day 1

A godly man in an ungodly world

> ➤ *Begin by reading Psalm 120.*
> ➤ *Pray about what you have read.*
> ➤ *Make notes on what you think God is teaching you.*
> ➤ *Read the chapter.*
> ➤ *Answer the questions in the section 'For your journal'.*

Psalm 120

Home is where the heart is. So the saying goes.
There is a Welsh word *'hiraeth'*, which is almost impossible to translate. It means an intense homesickness that can render the sufferer ill. There can exist a longing for familiar sights, sounds and smells of what memory calls 'home' that is intense. Something of that 'longing for home' is apparent in this opening psalm of ascent.

Jerusalem was the psalmist's 'home'. It is not that he *lived* there; it is rather that he longed *to be* there. It is quite likely that he had made pilgrimages to this city as a young boy. It was here that he met with his fellow Jews at the occasion of

the great feasts of Israel. More importantly, God himself had
made his 'home' here by coming to dwell in the temple. But
for some reason, the psalmist finds himself as far away from
Jerusalem as it was possible to get.

He talks about being in two places: 'Meshech', which is
thought to have been somewhere in the north, near the Black
Sea (in what we would regard as the Baltic Republics); and to
the south, 'among the tents of Kedar' in the Arabian desert
(v. 5). Whatever his precise geographical location, emotionally
and spiritually, he resides among the heathen: he feels far away
from God and from the comforting reassurance of Christian
fellowship. Unlike the sense of joy that opens Psalm 122, here
the psalmist is melancholic: saddened by days of deprivation
and opposition, he pines for better days to come. A spiritual
melancholy has enveloped him. He is singing 'the blues'.

Every now and then, most believers will find themselves
suffering from spiritual depression. When things don't go
according to *our* plan, we tend to get down. Something of this
dis-ease is reflected in the opening verse of this psalm: here is
a man who is in a state of 'distress' (v. 1; see 'woe', v. 5). 'The
Holy Spirit has exhorted the faithful', wrote John Calvin in a
comment on Psalm 47:1-2, 'to continue clapping their hands
for joy, until the advent of the promised Redeemer.'[1] But there
are times when we feel unable to comply with this sentiment.
The Psalms are nothing if not honest. And this psalm relates
with alarming frankness just how the psalmist felt. In so doing,
it accurately reflects the condition of many Christians who
find themselves in similar circumstances from time to time.

It probably goes without saying that Psalm 120 is not a
'favourite' psalm for most Christians. On the surface, it
is far too pessimistic and gloomy; it goes against the grain
of what we modern Christians are led to expect from our
faith. Conditions of deprivation and distress are not central

to modern expressions of Christianity. We are taught that singing 'I'm h-a-p-p-y' is essential to our faith. Christians who betray seriousness, or worse, melancholy, are living spiritually impoverished lives. What they need, we are informed, is a fresh baptism of the Spirit, an awakening to what Christianity is all about: unmixed pleasures and prosperity.

Those who propagate such views sometimes cite Scripture to support what they say. Does not the Bible teach that we can expect to receive 'a hundredfold now in this time' such things as 'houses and brothers and sisters and mothers and children and lands' (Mark 10:30)? Certainly there are Christians who have taken such verses quite literally, spreading a gospel of health and wealth as the rightful expectation of every believer, and with it an expectation that Christians should experience an unrelenting sense of joy, somewhat narrowly defined as something frothy and exterior.

The supporters of this view of the Christian life forget that Jesus adds a caveat: 'with persecutions' (Mark 10:30)! No part of our Christian experience in this world will be free from suffering in some form or another. Every Christian must expect to receive things he does not want, and to be denied things that he craves. 'Losses and crosses', to borrow a phrase from the Puritans, is part of our lot, no matter how far advanced in holiness we may be. It was a lesson the apostle Paul learned following his first missionary journey: 'through many tribulations we must enter the kingdom of God' (Acts 14:22). And when Christians find themselves up against the wall, facing the 'slings and arrows of outrageous fortune', it is understandable that they express a sense of sadness and near despair. One of the lessons that Jesus teaches us in his earthly life is that in the Garden of Gethsemane he came as close to despair as it is possible to get *without sinning*. Such intense seriousness was fitting for the occasion, and in displaying it,

our Lord sanctions such feelings in the lives of his children. It
is both dangerous and wrong to deny them.

The Bible is nothing if not completely candid about the
condition of some of its most well-known believers. There
are times when the best of God's people are downcast, when
all they can say is 'Woe is me!' There are occasions when the
light of God's countenance seems to be withdrawn and the
Christian believer has to walk about in the dark (Isa. 40:27;
49:14). The first of the Ascent Psalms seeks to identify with
this spiritual malaise and to minister to those who suffer from
it. It is, perhaps, encouraging in and of itself, that the Bible
recognizes the condition so transparently. If it teaches nothing
else, it tells us that those who feel like this are not alone.
Even some of God's giants have known times of anguish and
despair. The psalmist feels far away from the Lord and the
whole thing is getting him down.

Isolation from God is something which this psalm shares
in common with two others, Psalms 42 and 43. It is the
sense of isolation from God that caused the psalmist to be
downcast there too: 'These things I remember, as I pour out
my soul: how I would go with the throng and lead them in
procession to the house of God with glad shouts and songs
of praise, a multitude keeping festival' (Ps. 42:4). He had
been one of the Levitical singers in the choir at the temple,
accustomed to leading the congregation of Israel through
the temple gates in joyous celebration of their great religious
festivals. But now, physically separated from Jerusalem for
some reason, he can no longer participate in those jubilant
occasions. He is homesick for what had been the high point of
his experience.

The psalmist is not alone in these feelings.

Elijah knew spiritual depression. When he faced the
prophets of Baal and the ferocity of Ahab and Jezebel, he

found himself demonstrating the power of the God of Israel by a pyrotechnic display of fire. The water-drenched sacrifice ignited as soon as Elijah called upon God to show his power (1 Kings 18:21-39). And yet, within a few hours we find him sitting beneath a juniper tree, utterly dejected and wishing his life away (1 Kings 19:1-19).

Jonah, in very different circumstances, runs away from God's revealed will. Instead of going to Nineveh to preach a message of forgiveness and reconciliation, he found himself taking a course of action which would lead him in the very opposite direction. When, after God had caught up with him, Jonah repents and does as he is told, we find him sitting underneath a vine and feeling utterly sorry for himself. He says, 'It is better for me to die than to live' (Jonah 4:8).

The two disciples on the Emmaus Road, Cleopas and his companion (was it his wife, perhaps?), are a case in point (Luke 24:13-27). These two are walking the seven-mile journey to Emmaus having witnessed the death and burial of Jesus Christ. They were disappointed, depressed, and close to despair. All their hopes had been dashed to pieces in the events of the previous two or three days. They were going home, and every step of the journey seemed to be painful and wearisome. They even looked *sad* (v. 17).

Life is like that; it is about unfulfilled expectations, sudden providences with devastating, unexplained consequences. You plan ahead only to have those plans shattered by unforeseen events. 'In the world you will have tribulation,' Jesus warned (John 16:33). There is a war in which the Christian finds himself pitted against hostile forces determined to bring him down. The casualties of this conflict are the 'walking worried'. *And the psalmist seems to be one of them!*

What are the causes of this spiritual melancholy? Psalm 120 mentions two in particular.

1. *The opposition of the world.* No Christian is sheltered from the world's ill will. Just because Christians live the way they do, shunning the world's gratification of personal power, profit and pleasure, they can expect the world to hate them. What the psalmist mentions here, 'lying lips' and 'a deceitful tongue' (v. 2), is but the world's response when stung by the believer's refusal of its lifestyle. By building an ark, Noah 'condemned the world' (Heb. 11:7). We may, like the psalmist, desire peace; but the world has declared 'war' (v. 7).

Christians are the Lord's soldier-pilgrims and there is no advance made in the kingdom of God without opposition. The English puritan, John Geree, wrote in a tract, *The Character of an Old English Puritane or Non-conformist* (1646), 'His whole life he accounted a warfare, wherein Christ was his captain, his arms, prayers and tears. The cross his banner and his word [motto]: *Vincit qui patitur* [he who suffers, conquers].'[2] It is opposition of this kind that produced in the Puritans such sharpness of wisdom and refinement of discipleship. In God's overall plan, opposition and difficulty are meant for our 'good' (Rom. 8:28).

This is what Jesus tells us to expect. Unbelievers, Jesus warns, will know nothing of the world's opposition: 'If the world hates you, know that it has hated me before it hated you. If you were of the world, the world would love you as its own; but because you are not of the world, but I chose you out of the world, therefore the world hates you' (John 15:18-19). Whether the opposition is cool and calculating, or fervent and ferocious, the effect is the same.

Christians who refuse to falsify data, steal from the company, or condone the sexual liaisons of a modern working environment can expect to be ridiculed, even despised. Promotions may be bypassed in favour of someone who willingly complies with the world's expectations. I think of a businessman who, when asked to display his product at a prestigious exhibition in London, complied but refused to open his stand on the Lord's Day — the busiest day of all. Though there was admiration from some, bemusement by others, there was equally a sense of outrage, for the act had appeared to condemn the unprincipled standards of the world. This is part of what we can expect, and Peter warns us not to be surprised when trials of this sort come upon us suddenly (1 Peter 4:12).

> God can look sourly, and chide bitterly, and strike heavily, even where and when he loves dearly. The hand of God was very much against Job, and yet his love, his heart, was very much set upon Job... The hand of God was sore against David and Jonah, when his heart was much set upon them. He that shall conclude that the heart of God is against those that his hand is against will condemn the generation of the just, whom God unjustly would not have condemned.
>
> Thomas Brooks, *Precious Remedies against Satan's Devices*[3]

It is interesting that the psalmist is the subject of malicious talk. So was John Bunyan. Making his way to a service on horseback in the pouring rain, he noticed a young girl whom he recognized as heading to the same service. In giving her a ride on the horse certain people gossiped, accusing the preacher of impropriety. The tale followed him for many years and was the cause of much distress.

Sadly, tale-bearers are to be found in the church also. It is one reason why James warns us that the tongue is 'a fire, a world of unrighteousness ... set among our members, staining the whole body, setting on fire the entire course of life, and set on fire by hell' (James 3:6).

Hostility is, of course, what Jesus experienced: an uncomprehending family, an unsympathetic government, and even friends who betrayed him. Lies and deceit were the cause of his crucifixion. And it is this fact alone — that in experiencing the hostility of the world we are at the same time following in the footsteps of our Master — which strengthens and motivates us to persevere.

2. *The allurement of the world.* Complaining as he does that he has lived among the heathen for too long (vv. 5-6), the psalmist seems to raise a quite different problem. The world is more than just hostile and antagonistic to the believer. There is a quite different and far more subtle danger: that of yielding to the world's allurement. One of Satan's ploys is to undermine the believer's holiness by compromising his lifestyle. Believers are to pursue holiness, an internal and external conformity to be like Christ. The constant pressure of the world is such that it prevents this process of change from taking place, and it may be that the psalmist was aware of the world's stamp upon his current lifestyle. The sanctifying effect of rubbing shoulders with other believers had been withdrawn.

It is the eternal purpose of the triune God to conform his people to the image of Christ. No one saw it clearer than Peter, who having failed Christ dismally on several occasions, insisted that believers are chosen 'according to the foreknowledge of God the Father, in the sanctification of the Spirit, for obedience to Jesus Christ and for sprinkling with his blood' (1 Peter 1:2). By way of incentives he adds that God himself is holy and that we are to be like him (v. 15), that Christ died in order to purchase holiness for us (vv. 18-19), and that we must all meet God as our Judge and give an account of ourselves (v. 17). Living a worldly life frustrates the counsels of the triune God whose aim is to purify us and make us like his Son.

Perhaps the psalmist is conscious that the distinctive qualities of holiness are missing from his life. In taking stock of his current spiritual condition he notices the elements of compromise. It is a time of leanness. He thinks about the joy of worshipping God in Jerusalem and *he misses it!*

It has to be said at once that this is a good sign. People who don't miss spiritual things when they are forcibly kept away for one reason or another are in bad shape. If we can be absent from worship for no good reason and not miss it, we are in a dangerous condition, a hair's breadth away from catastrophe. Why was the psalmist far away from Jerusalem? He may have had a perfectly good reason, but perhaps he had moved there quite deliberately because of some worldly advantage. Perhaps he had entertained the idea that he was strong enough to survive without regular visits to the place of worship. Perhaps, like some Hebrew Christians in the New Testament, assembling together with other believers was something he had begun to regard as unnecessary (Heb. 10:25). Such notions are, of course, quite wrong.

The way of recovery

When we find ourselves in similar circumstances to that of the psalmist, how can we cope? What can we do to remedy the situation? The answer seems to lie in recognizing five important truths.

Firstly, it is important to recognize that *an enemy exists.* It is always fatal to underestimate the power of an enemy bent on our destruction. The psalmist was not about to make that mistake. His enemy was a liar, one who had declared war.

It would be foolish to ignore his threats. It is a lesson that Christians fail to learn to their cost. It is so easy to downplay the threat that the world, or indwelling sin, or the devil himself poses. To pretend that the forces of darkness are inconsequential can prove to be the means of our destruction. In dealing with indwelling sin, for example, Paul assumes that we have recognized our need to deal with sin and that we have the means to do so when he exhorts his readers, 'For if you live according to the flesh you will die, but if by the Spirit you put to death the deeds of the body, you will live' (Rom. 8:13).

Secondly, it is equally important to recognize *our inadequacy to overcome our enemy*. Just as Paul encourages mortification *by the power of the indwelling Spirit* in Romans 8:13, so the psalmist finds himself unable to cope. He is in 'distress' (v. 1). The Christian life is never easy, and saints down through the ages have confessed their weakness in the face of the enemy. The New Testament warns the one who thinks he is strong, 'take heed lest he fall' (1 Cor. 10:12). Jesus said, 'Those who are well have no need of a physician, but those who are sick' (Matt. 9:12).

This leads to a third truth: a recognition that *the source of all our hope lies in the power of God*. It is in the name of the 'LORD' (v. 1) that the psalmist finds renewed strength and motivation in his melancholy. This is the very name that had enlivened Moses' faith when asked to return to Egypt knowing that a price lay on his head (Exod. 3:15). There is a hymn which includes the lines:

The arm of flesh will fail you,
    You dare not trust your own.[4]

George Duffield Jr
1818-1888

That is why the psalmist begins with a plea to God to come and help him: 'In my distress I called to the LORD' (v. 1). It is because he has realized his weakness that he cries to the Lord to save and deliver him.

At one point in the psalm he confronts his enemy and warns him of the consequences of his malice. His words of enmity may well have hurt the psalmist, but they are as nothing in comparison with the judgement that this enemy will receive from God. As weapons, the psalmist's enemy has used words, likened to 'sharp arrows' and 'glowing coals' (v. 4; the roots of the 'broom tree' apparently burn well and make good charcoal). These metaphors pick up allusions elsewhere in the Old Testament: 'A man who bears false witness against his neighbour is like a war club, or a sword, or a sharp arrow' (Prov. 25:18); 'A worthless man plots evil, and his speech is like a scorching fire' (Prov. 16:27). In the judgement, the justice of God will see to it that like is met with like: arrows will be met with arrows and fire with fire. Something similar is found in an earlier psalm:

> But God shoots his arrow at them;
> > they are wounded suddenly.
> They are brought to ruin, with their own tongues
> > turned against them;
> all who see them will wag their heads
>
> > (Ps. 64:7-8).

This is what the psalmist does, then, when he finds himself in trouble: he confronts his enemy and tells him what God is going to do! It was David's tactic when confronting Goliath. He said to him, 'You come to me with a sword and with a spear and with a javelin, but I come to you in the name of the LORD of hosts, the God of the armies of Israel, whom you have defied' (1 Sam. 17:45). It was also the strength that Gideon gained against the Midianites: 'A sword for the LORD and for Gideon!' (Judg. 7:20). It is for this very reason that the apostle Paul encourages Christians to be strong 'in the Lord and in the strength of his might' (Eph. 6:10). It is the only way to confront the enemy: armed with the power of God!

It is at once a confidence in God's sovereignty and power to which the psalmist has recourse. What does the knowledge of God's sovereignty imply? It implies many things, including the reassurance that his purposes cannot fail (Isa. 46:9-10; Dan. 4:34-35). If God is not sovereign he cannot be God! It was this very truth that helped Job in his trials: 'I know that you can do all things, and that no purpose of yours can be thwarted' (Job 42:2). Even the cruel actions of the psalmist's enemies were part of God's overall plan and purpose — something that the Bible witnesses to in Job's trials (Job 2:3), as well as in the greatest of all crimes: the death of Christ himself (Acts 2:23). The explanation is given by Joseph, who had himself suffered at the hands of his own brothers' evil intent, 'you meant evil against me, but God meant it for good, to bring it about that many people should be kept alive' (Gen. 50:20).

> 'From my childhood up,' wrote Jonathan Edwards, 'my mind had been full of objections against the doctrine of God's sovereignty... It used to appear like a horrible doctrine to me. But I remember the time very well, when I seemed to be convinced, and fully satisfied, as to this sovereignty of God... I have often since had not only a conviction but a delightful conviction. The doctrine has very often appeared exceeding pleasant, bright, and sweet. Absolute sovereignty is what I love to ascribe to God.'[5]

Knowing God as the King of our lives is the way out of spiritual melancholy.

Truth number four is that *prayer is the key that unlocks the gate to renewed fellowship with God.* It appears as though the psalmist had known God's help on many an occasion in the past. The opening verse is a testimony to the benefit of answered prayer: 'In my distress I called to the LORD, and he answered me. Deliver me, O LORD...' (vv. 1-2). His expectation of God's help *now* is based on the experience of knowing his help on previous occasions. The way out of his despondency and gloom is to have recourse to prayer. Fellowship with God in prayer is the means by which his strength is renewed.

We are to pray at all times (1 Thess. 5:17). That means that we are to pray at every significant moment, making the most of every opportunity. This is especially good advice when we find ourselves in trouble of any kind. Just as police need constantly to keep in touch with headquarters so that their whereabouts might be known, and that they in turn may pass on information, so the Christian needs to keep in constant touch with the Lord. When Nehemiah sent up an 'arrow-like' prayer when he was asked to explain his demeanour to King Artaxerxes, his instant recourse to prayer *at that moment* was the result of a habit of disciplined prayer (Neh. 2:1-4; compare 1:4). It is the same here. The psalmist knows from previous occasions that 'prayer works'.

> When all things seem against us, to drive us to despair
> We know one gate is open, one ear will hear our prayer.[6]

Prayer is a renewal of fellowship with God. By vocalizing the condition of our souls before the Lord we are reminded that he came into this world in the person of Jesus Christ. By prayer we are reminded of our Sin-bearer and Substitute who is able to 'sympathize with our weaknesses' (Heb. 4:15). 'For because he himself has suffered when tempted, he is able to help those who are being tempted' (Heb. 2:18).

Being serious about his enemy, his need, and God's sovereign power to which he has recourse through prayer, the psalmist finds the beginnings of his release from spiritual depression. The journey which he now takes, a journey that we will follow in these psalms, is one which will lead to the very greatest of spiritual blessings. There is a way out of spiritual depression and it begins by honestly facing up to our present condition. If you find yourself in similar circumstances to the psalmist then begin by acknowledging it. Do more than that! Go and tell God all about it! *Tell him everything!*

Maybe before we can do that, we need to ask ourselves whether we miss the presence of God in our lives as much as the psalmist did. Perhaps we need to pray first, 'Lord make me thirsty for yourself.' If a bout of spiritual depression will bring you to pray a prayer like that, you will have cause to turn around and thank God for it!

There is one final truth — the prayer isn't answered! More accurately, it *is* answered, but not in the way we might have expected. Recognizing this — that God makes us wait for his blessings — is part of the remedy to despair. The pilgrim remains in a dark place at the end of the psalm, but armed now with fresh resolve. Darkness had brought out some steeliness in soul. In saying, 'not *yet*', God has strengthened him for the harsher battles of life.

For your journal...

1. Why are some psalms more appealing to you than others? As you think about this, consider whether an imbalance has crept into your life because you have failed to appreciate the breadth of spirituality expressed in the book of Psalms.

2. Do you know what it means to be discouraged? Are there particular issues that constantly get you down? What are they?

3. If the motto *Vincit qui patitur* (he who suffers, conquers) is true, how should this affect the way you view your life as a Christian?

4. Have you been absent from corporate worship recently? Are there good reasons for this absence? Is this a sign of backsliding?

Psalm 121

A Song of Ascents

1   *I lift up my eyes to the hills.*
     From where does my help come?
2   *My help comes from the LORD,*
     who made heaven and earth.

3   *He will not let your foot be moved;*
     he who keeps you will not slumber.
4   *Behold, he who keeps Israel*
     will neither slumber nor sleep.

5   *The LORD is your keeper;*
     the LORD is your shade on your right hand.
6   *The sun shall not strike you by day,*
     nor the moon by night.

7   *The LORD will keep you from all evil;*
     he will keep your life.
8   *The LORD will keep*
     your going out and your coming in
     from this time forth and for evermore.

Day 2

Needing help

➢ *Begin by reading Psalm 121.*
➢ *Pray about what you have read.*
➢ *Make notes on what you think God is teaching you.*
➢ *Read the chapter.*
➢ *Answer the questions in the section 'For your journal'.*

Imagine a group of pilgrims making their way to Jerusalem, ascending the range of 'hills' (121:1) that surround the ancient city. Potentially, these hills hide bandits and marauders out to rob unsuspecting families preoccupied with thoughts of worship. At such times, the overriding need is a trust in a sovereign, protecting Lord. *God watches over his own people.*

This psalm reassures us of God's covenant care at all times, in every conceivable situation. It has proved to be a favourite psalm of a great many believers through the ages. William Romaine, the eighteenth-century preacher and friend of George Whitefield, is said to have read this psalm every day! There is no doubt that its truths can change *our* lives. By challenging our fears and unbelief, this psalm helps us to focus upon the Lord in a new way. In these lines we are assured of the divine companion who is at our right hand every moment of the day.

Journeys are potentially crisis-laden, then as now, and the knowledge of a guiding hand is reassuring. Older translations of this psalm's opening lines seem to indicate that the psalmist found safety by hiding in the hills that surround Jerusalem. But, undoubtedly, the hills were the problem, not the solution, for in these hills all kinds of thieves and robbers were lying in wait to plunder unsuspecting pilgrims. Their safety was found in the Lord himself who protected them from what the hills might be concealing.

It is the plaintive question, 'From where does my help come?', that echoes in our own souls (121:1). It reminds us of another psalm, one written in a time of great distress, and which begins in this way:

> Hear my prayer, O LORD;
> let my cry come to you!
> Do not hide your face from me
>   in the day of my distress!
> Incline your ear to me;
>   answer me speedily in the day when I call!

> (Ps. 102:1-2).

The answer to this cry (it is one that occurs over fifty times in the Psalms) is a God-centred one: 'My help comes from the LORD' (121:2). It, too, is a cry we hear more than once:

> Our soul waits for the LORD;
>   he is our help and our shield

> (Ps. 33:20).

Our help is in the name of the Lord,
    who made heaven and earth

(Ps. 124:8).

This gives rise to the idea that there are two 'voices' in this psalm. On the one hand, there is the cry of a fearful, inexperienced believer who is frightened that his feet will slip, frightened of the noon-day sun, of the moon and especially of robbers. On the other hand, there is the reassuring cry of a more confident voice which singles out truths about God that directly impinge upon such fears. The experienced, more mature believer is answering the fearful cries of the inexperienced and less mature believer. The former is saying to the latter: *Trust in God — every step of the way! Learn to appreciate what kind of God he is!*

A covenant presence

Psalm 121 is reassuring from the perspective of the covenant. The capitalization of the name 'Lord' in verse 2 is a custom in our English Bibles for designating the specific name, Yahweh (sometimes rendered YHWH, and in older English translations, 'Jehovah').[1] It might best be thought of as 'Covenant Lord', since it was a name given in the context of God's promise to Moses of a name by which he could be identified by the people of God held in bondage in Egypt. In Exodus 3, Moses is being commissioned to return to Egypt and deliver his brothers and sisters from their captivity. Naturally, in the face of this daunting task he asks for a name by which the Lord may be identified by the people. The response is a strange one: 'I AM WHO I AM,' then shortened to just, 'I AM', is the one who will deliver them (Exod. 3:14). The answer to the

question, 'From where does my help come?', is the verb 'to
be'! God is making a point: earlier in the Exodus narrative, he
had told Moses, 'I will be with you' (Exod. 3:12). What is God
saying? He is saying this: in the midst of the trials that are to
come (and there *will be* trials), 'I AM ... *with you!*' What could
be more reassuring than that? The name that identifies God
to the Israelites is one which reassures them of his continual
presence.

> God also said to Moses, 'Say this to the people of
> Israel, "The LORD, the God of your fathers, the God of
> Abraham, the God of Isaac, and the God of Jacob, has
> sent me to you." This is my name for ever, and thus I am
> to be remembered throughout all generations'
>
> (Exod. 3:15).

The significance of this name becomes apparent as the
history of redemption progresses. Time and again, the
expression, 'I will be with you' is repeated (Gen. 26:3; 31:3;
Josh. 1:5; Judg. 6:16; 1 Kings 11:38; Isa. 43:2). Sometimes,
it is found in another form: 'He will not leave you or forsake
you' (Deut. 31:8; cf. Josh. 1:5; 1 Chr. 28:20; 2 Chr. 15:2;
Heb. 13:5). In the pages of the New Testament it finds its
fulfilment in Jesus Christ, Immanuel, which means 'God with
us' (Matt. 1:23).

It is breathtaking that John, for example, should begin his
account of the life of Jesus in the way that he does. As a Jew,
John adhered to the most fundamental of Jewish truths about
God: that he is *one* (Deut. 6:4). The *Shema*, as this assertion
was referred to, formed the daily affirmation of every godly
Jew. The translation of the Hebrew Scriptures current in
John's time rendered the divine name of God as *Kurios*. It
is astonishing, then, that John should say in the opening few

lines of his Gospel that Jesus is *Kurios* (John 1:1). *Jesus is
Lord! Jesus is Yahweh.*

Losing the sense of God's presence made the journey to
Jerusalem harder. What sustained the psalmist in the hours of
turmoil and anxiety was a certainty that God was with him.

> For what great nation is there that has a god so near to
> it as the Lord our God is to us, whenever we call upon
> him?
>
> (Deut. 4:7).

> Blessed are the people who know the festal shout,
>   who walk, O Lord, in the light of your face
>
> (Ps. 89:15).

Sometimes our guilt hurts so much that we madly want
to do something extraordinary to make the pain stop. But
what does God require of us for our spiritual recovery?
Simple: renewed obedience in his means of killing the
flesh. His means are those outlined throughout his Word
and they're familiar: constantly reading his Word, hearing
it preached, and reflecting on it; fervent prayer; careful
watching against temptation; and fixing the mind always
on things above, where Christ is seated at the right hand
of God.

Kris Lundgaard, *Through the Looking Glass*[2]

Sovereign Creator

Not only is God identified as a covenant presence; he is also the
One who 'made heaven and earth' (121:2). The threats which
arise on the journey to Jerusalem arise within a world the Lord

has made and which he sustains. In *this* world — not in some imaginary, idealistic world — God reigns supreme and triumphant. There is nothing in the world that threatens his rule.

In the discussions that abound over the relationship of science and religion, particularly in the area of the age of the earth, it is easy to lose sight of the immense pastoral implications of the doctrine of creation. The sovereign power that creates the universe in all its complexity is the power that now offers support in the difficulties in which we find ourselves. In the beginning, there was nothing apart from God in all his incomprehensible glory. Out of nothing (*ex nihilo*) he brought into being all that is. The God who made man sustains him in every circumstance. There is no set of contingencies that threatens God in any way.

> Why do you say, O Jacob,
>   and speak, O Israel,
> 'My way is hidden from the LORD,
>   and my right is disregarded by my God'?
> Have you not known? Have you not heard?
> The LORD is the everlasting God,
>   the Creator of the ends of the earth.
> He does not faint or grow weary;
>   his understanding is unsearchable.
> He gives power to the faint,
>   and to him who has no might he increases strength.
> Even youths shall faint and be weary,
>   and young men shall fall exhausted;
> but they who wait for the LORD shall renew their strength;
>   they shall mount up with wings like eagles;
> they shall run and not be weary;
>   they shall walk and not faint

(Isa. 40:27-31).

The Creator sustains! The Creator strengthens! The Creator *keeps*!

> ...he who *keeps* you will not slumber.
> Behold, he who *keeps* Israel
>   will neither slumber nor sleep.

> The LORD is your *keeper*...

> The LORD will *keep* you from all evil;
>   he will *keep* your life.
> The LORD will *keep*
>   your going out and your coming in
>   from this time forth and for evermore
> > (Ps. 121:3b-8, emphasis mine).

Six times God says he will keep us safe and secure. Whatever the threat may be, God keeps his covenant people safe, in a personal and collective sense (121:1-4). Round the clock, God's vigils protect his own from real and imaginary dangers (121:5-6). He keeps 'for evermore' (121:8).

i. God is never out of touch

> ...he who *keeps* you will not slumber.
> Behold, he who *keeps* Israel
>   will neither slumber nor sleep
> > (Ps. 121:3-4, emphasis mine).

Do you remember how Elijah taunted the prophets of Baal on Mount Carmel, suggesting that their god might be asleep? (1 Kings 18:27). But the God of Israel never sleeps! He never loses consciousness of his people. He is ever awake to our

needs. He who has redeemed Israel is not going to lose him
on the way home (Exod. 6:8). Knowing that the Lord is never
inaccessible, or 'too busy' to deal with our particular case,
is what makes the Christian life so wonderfully refreshing.
Perhaps the psalmist was thinking in verse 3 of the possibility
of losing one's footing on the way to Jerusalem and falling
into a ravine without anyone noticing. But, God would notice!
Whatever befalls us, we can be assured of God's presence
throughout the journey home.

ii. God provides shelter along the way

> The LORD is your keeper;
>   the LORD is your *shade* on your right hand.
> The sun shall not strike you by day,
>   nor the moon by night
>   (Ps. 121:5-6, emphasis mine).

Why be afraid of the sun and moon? The threat of
heatstroke from excessive sunlight is a serious one on a
journey like this. But, what of the moon? Could it be that
the dangers here were imaginary rather than real? We know
only too well that sometimes our imagination can trouble
us more than reality. We imagine dangers that are not there.
The film industry has played on this fear to its very limit,
introducing darkness and shadows, eerie noises and perceived
expectations that can cause us to tremble and fear. The moon
was also associated, then as now, with lunacy. God protects us
from those forces which unhinge the mind. He keeps us sane
in a mad world.

God will provide the shelter that will assure us of a safe
journey home. It is the cry of the psalmist again and again.

Keep me as the apple of your eye;
    hide me in the shadow of your wings

                                (Ps. 17:8).

How precious is your steadfast love, O God!
    The children of mankind take refuge in the shadow of
        your wings

                                (Ps. 36:7).

Be merciful to me, O God, be merciful to me,
    for in you my soul takes refuge;
in the shadow of your wings I will take refuge,
    till the storms of destruction pass by

                                (Ps. 57:1).

iii. God keeps us secure

The LORD will *keep* you from all evil;
    he will *keep* your life.
The LORD will *keep*
    your going out and your coming in
    from this time forth and for evermore
                (Ps. 121:7-8, emphasis mine).

Have you noticed how the psalm has made progress from
the small steps (slipping feet in verse 3) to the whole of life
(the comings and goings in verse 8)? In the totality of life there
is no opposition that can finally crush us.

For I am sure that neither death nor life, nor angels
nor rulers, nor things present nor things to come, nor
powers, nor height nor depth, nor anything else in all

creation, will be able to separate us from the love of God in Christ Jesus our Lord

(Rom. 8:38-39).

There is a story told of an Atlantic crossing made in the nineteenth century from Liverpool, England, to New York. In the middle of the night the ship was tossed about by a fierce storm which woke everyone aboard, including a little girl. Many had begun to get dressed fearing the worst, but the girl asked a steward who had entered her room, 'Is father on deck?'

'Yes,' came the reply, at which point she got back into bed and fell fast asleep again.

This is the confidence of all who know their heavenly Father. He watches over us from above; and we are safe in his arms.

For your journal…

1. Reflect on God's covenant and write down every blessing that you can think of that results from it. Spend time praising God for these blessings.

2. 'Losing the sense of God's presence made the journey to Jerusalem harder.' How does this apply to your own life?

3. Think about how vast the universe is. Remind yourself that God made all of it, and he made you! How should you respond to this knowledge?

4. Can you think of some of the ways in which God has kept you from falling recently? What have you done to acknowledge this kindness?

Psalm 122

A Song of Ascents. Of David.

1   I was glad when they said to me,
        'Let us go to the house of the LORD!'
2   Our feet have been standing
        within your gates, O Jerusalem!

3   Jerusalem — built as a city
        that is bound firmly together,
4   to which the tribes go up,
        the tribes of the LORD,
    as was decreed for Israel,
        to give thanks to the name of the LORD.
5   There thrones for judgement were set,
        the thrones of the house of David.

6   Pray for the peace of Jerusalem!
        'May they be secure who love you!
7   Peace be within your walls
        and security within your towers!'
8   For my brothers and companions' sake
        I will say, 'Peace be within you!'
9   For the sake of the house of the LORD our God,
        I will seek your good.

Day 3

Jerusalem

> ➤ *Begin by reading Psalm 122.*
> ➤ *Pray about what you have read.*
> ➤ *Make notes on what you think God is teaching you.*
> ➤ *Read the chapter.*
> ➤ *Answer the questions in the section 'For your journal'.*

Psalm 122

At last, the psalmist has arrived in Jerusalem!

> Our feet have been standing
>   within your gates, O Jerusalem!
>
> (Ps. 122:2).

'The sight will never be blotted from the book of memory,' wrote one twentieth-century visitor on seeing Jerusalem for the first time. Recalling some words from Wordsworth, he continues: 'In coming days I expect it "to flash upon that inward eye which is the bliss of solitude", and when that happens, the heart will again thrill with the pleasure of it.'[1]

Of this city, it would be said:

> beautiful in elevation,
>   is the joy of all the earth
>
> (Ps. 48:2).

During the Babylonian exile, one writer could exclaim on seeing the ruins of Jerusalem:

> All who pass along the way
>   clap their hands at you;
> they hiss and wag their heads
>   at the daughter of Jerusalem;
> 'Is this the city that was called
>   the perfection of beauty,
>   the joy of all the earth?'
>
> (Lam. 2:15).

'The perfection of beauty!' A higher claim could not be made.

The city — at last!

It is difficult for us to imagine the emotions that would have been released as these pilgrims arrived in Jerusalem, the City of God. For pilgrims from the country, and especially the diaspora, city-life had a measure of excitement and energy that was altogether different from the tranquil existence of rural life. Real life is in the city, people think. In the Old Testament, there was more truth to this than we may imagine. God's covenant presence, which the previous psalm had anticipated, was to be found in Jerusalem in a particular way. *The temple was there*!

For the Old Testament believer, Jerusalem was the place where God resided. No other place on earth could claim for itself this distinction: 'the place that the LORD your God will choose ... to make his name dwell there' (Deut. 12:5,11; compare 26:2). Jerusalem (formerly the ancient Canaanite city of Jebus) was captured by David (2 Sam. 5:6-10), and after Solomon built the temple on its most prominent location, the city gained a unique spiritual significance: 'For the sake of the house of the LORD our God, I will seek your good' (Ps. 122:9). It explains why believers longed to be there. God had 'chosen Zion' (Ps. 132:13). 'He chose ... Mount Zion, which he loves. He built his sanctuary like the high heavens, like the earth, which he has founded for ever' (Ps. 78:68-69).

When David brought the ark of the covenant from Shiloh to Jerusalem (2 Sam. 6), he ensured that Jerusalem became the City of God. The ark contained the Tables of the Law (Deut. 10:5; 31:9), and its position within the temple at Jerusalem was a vivid reminder of the covenant made with Israel at Sinai (Exod. 25:22). At the very heart of the city of Jerusalem was a reminder that *God had spoken!*

The significance of Jerusalem was not erased by the division of Israel in the time of Jeroboam. Despite his attempts to make Dan and Bethel centres of worship for the northern kingdom, the faithful still flocked to Jerusalem, 'to which the tribes go up, the tribes of the LORD, as was decreed for Israel' (Ps. 122:4). As this psalm suggests, Jerusalem was the centre of Israel's life; it was here that judgements were made and justice dispensed (v. 5); it was here that the most holy festivals were kept; it was here that God had made a home. A prayer an Israelite might utter would be, 'that I may dwell in the house of the LORD all the days of my life, to gaze upon the beauty of the LORD and to enquire in his temple' (Ps. 27:4).

During the four centuries from David to Nebuchadnezzar, Jerusalem knew times of prosperity — though never such as to match the glories of the days of Solomon. One event stood out, an event which cultivated in some a belief that the city would be defended at all costs. Under the siege of the city by Sennacherib, the Assyrian army was dealt a severe and fatal blow which sent it home (2 Kings 19:35-37). Some concluded that Jerusalem was invincible and boasted appropriately (Jer. 7:7). The arrogance — for such it was — was quickly shattered. Shortly afterwards, Jerusalem became subject, first to Assyria and then to Babylon, who eventually razed the city to the ground and exiled its people (2 Kings 25; Jer. 52).

Jerusalem and its temple had become a matter of super-stition. Instead of trusting in the Lord, people had given their hearts to bricks and mortar, stones and wood. It was a deviation that God was bound to put right. And when the destruction came, the reaction of God's people was one of devastation. Asaph was heard to cry, 'O God, the nations have come into your inheritance; they have defiled your holy temple; they have laid Jerusalem in ruins' (Ps. 79:1; compare 74:5-8). Such laments turned to prayer: 'You will arise and have pity on Zion; it is the time to favour her; the appointed time has come. For your servants hold her stones dear and have pity on her dust' (Ps. 102:13-14); and again: 'If I forget you, O Jerusalem, let my right hand forget its skill! Let my tongue stick to the roof of my mouth, if I do not remember you, if I do not set Jerusalem above my highest joy!' (Ps. 137:5-6).

But, how should *we* view all this? What is the significance of Jerusalem *to us*?

Jerusalem takes on an even deeper significance in the New Testament. Our fascination, too, is with a city called Jeru-salem, not the ancient city of Old Testament times, or the one

Jesus visited, which the Romans destroyed in A.D. 70. It is a 'new Jerusalem' that we look for, a 'city that is to come' (Heb. 13:14), 'Jerusalem above ... our mother' (Gal. 4:26). It is a city without a temple, 'And I saw no temple in the city, for its temple is the Lord God the Almighty and the Lamb. And the city has no need of sun or moon to shine on it, for the glory of God gives it light, and its lamp is the Lamb. By its light will the nations walk, and the kings of the earth will bring their glory into it' (Rev. 21:22-24).

> There is a sweet sight of God in the face of a friend; for though the comfort given by God's messengers be ordinarily most effectual, as the blessing of parents, who are in God's room, is more effectual than the blessing of others upon their children, yet God hath promised a blessing to the offices of communion of saints performed by one private man towards another.
>
> Richard Sibbes, 'The Soul's Conflict with Itself', in *Works*[2]

We too should know the joy of belonging to this city, the thrill of entering the place where God's presence is known, his Word supplied, his grace promised. In part, this realization is ours by faith in Christ, but its full realization awaits the dawning of the new heavens and new earth, where God's people will gather to worship the Davidic king, Jesus Christ. Whenever we gather together for worship in the church of Jesus Christ, we anticipate a little of that fulness. With the Old Testament saints, we also 'rejoice' in anticipation (122:1, NIV).

- Do you know this joy?
- Has the joy of being a Christian subsided?
- Has the joy of worship evaporated?

When revival came to Jerusalem in the days that followed the exile, and the people wept on account of their sins, Nehemiah urged them to rejoice, saying, 'The joy of the LORD is your strength' (Neh. 8:10). When Paul tried to account for his own troubles and the perplexities that his beloved Philippian friends were experiencing at the thought of Paul's imprisonment, he too urged them to 'Rejoice in the Lord always; again I will say, Rejoice!' (Phil. 4:4). When the Westminster Divines sought to encapsulate the goal of the Christian life in one sentence (a daunting task!), they insisted upon saying that joy was a part of it: 'Man's chief end is to glorify God and [in so doing] to *enjoy* him for ever.' Joy was God's plan from the very beginning!

That is why the Lord's prayer for us is so illuminating: 'But now I am coming to you, and these things I speak in the world, that they may have my joy fulfilled in themselves' (John 17:13). Jesus prays that we might experience *joy*! — joy in worship, joy in corporate fellowship, joy in knowing that God loves us, joy in the assurance of his abiding presence with us, joy in knowing that we shall never be separated from him.

Streets, walls and buildings

One can easily imagine the psalmist doing what any tourist might do in a city, admiring the architecture and layout of its great buildings. In this case, it is the very structure of the city that is fascinating. The massive, fortress-like walls of the temple must have been impressive to country folk, used to canvas tents and hamlets. Three features stand out: *density*, *diversity* and *direction*.

Density. 'Jerusalem — built as a city that is bound firmly together' (Ps. 122:3). The economy of space in the city was noticeable to a countryman used, as he was, to wide open spaces. It is the thing such folk notice still about city life, how close together people live. The city of Jerusalem seemed firmly bound together. The very layout of the city seemed to speak of unity of purpose and goal. As such, it served as a model of what the kingdom of God ought always to be like. It is the *unity* of the city that seems to dominate here.

Diversity. It is particularly interesting that the psalm should highlight two features of the city that seem in contradiction to each other. After noticing its unity, it stresses its diversity: 'the tribes go up, the tribes of the LORD' (Ps. 122:4). The tribes of Israel were a disparate lot! There were the coastal dwellers of Zebulun, the highlanders of Dan, the farmers of Ephraim, and the desert dwellers of Reuben. Jerusalem would have been as fascinating to observe for its many accents as it would have been for its varied architecture! Sameness or total uniformity is something only the cults have sought after; within the community of God's people there has always been a recognition of the value of diversity. There are, to cite Paul, hands and feet, knees and elbows within God's church: 'the whole body, joined and held together by every joint with which it is equipped, when each part is working properly, makes the body grow so that it builds itself up in love' (Eph. 4:16). Such diversity ensures, as he tells us earlier in this epistle, the disclosure of the manifold wisdom of God (Eph. 3:10).

Direction. Issues of justice were often resolved in the ancient world at the city gate. There, the elders would gather to consider their verdict. It is what the psalm alludes to in verse 5: 'There thrones for judgement were set, the thrones of the house of David.' Quarrels were settled, disputes were resolved, and justice sought within these ancient walls. And here in Jerusalem, like no other city, the king resided! It is like visiting Washington and driving past the White House; or visiting London, and taking a bus tour to see Buckingham Palace! David's throne was coincident with the city of Jerusalem. It was from there that his word was issued, his will made known.

From a vantage point *before* the exile, Isaiah describes a day when pilgrims will return after the exile to Jerusalem and find safety within the 'strong city' (Isa. 26:1). They will call out for its doors to open wide and receive them (26:2). We, too, have our feet standing in this city according to the perspective of the New Testament. 'But you have come to Mount Zion and to the city of the living God' (Heb. 12:22). We come to a different city; but we, like the ancient Israelites, notice the unity and diversity of the people of God that make up the city's occupants and wait with eager expectation upon the Word of the King. It was the 'other-worldly' beauty of this city that John Newton (1725-1807) captured in his hymn, 'Glorious Things of Thee are Spoken', and especially the lines:

> Saviour, since of Zion's city
> I through grace a member am,
> Let the world deride or pity,
> I will glory in Thy name.
> Fading is the worldling's pleasure,
> All his boasted pomp and show;
> Solid joys and lasting treasure
> None but Zion's children know.

Do we have this sense of belonging to what Augustine called *The City of God*?

Peace, perfect peace!

'Pray for the peace of Jerusalem!' (Ps. 122:6). These words constitute a prayer that, according to one commentator, Jerusalem 'might live up to its name'. The 'salem' part of the city's name is a form of 'shalom', meaning 'peace'. At the heart of the psalm rises a desire for the well-being of the city. It is interesting to think that perhaps it was this very psalm that Jesus had in mind when he expressed a longing that the city might know those things that would bring her peace, namely *himself* (Luke 19:42).

What does the psalmist pray for, exactly? A threefold use of 'within' (vv. 7 [twice], 8) gives us the clue. Inner peace, a freedom from division *within* rather than a fear of what may come from outside, seems to be uppermost in his mind. It is the fear of inner disharmony and division. It is the welfare of 'brothers and companions' (122:8) and 'the house of the LORD our God' (122:9) that concerns him. Division hurts the people of God, individually; but it hurts *the body*, too. We ought to be concerned about the unity of the church of Jesus Christ, it seems to be saying.

The psalm ends with a resolution: 'I will seek your good' (122:9). It is the dedication of a heart touched by the mercies of God, and the joy of fellowship that results from it. It is the resolution of one who is prepared to give everything for the sake of the kingdom of God. Here is self-denial and singleness of motive in a Godward direction. It is the worshipper saying, '*I* want to be the answer to my own prayer: *I* will labour for the good of the kingdom of God. *I* will live and die with God's glory in view.'

Saint Columba, a sixth-century Irish missionary to the west of Scotland, prayed in this way:

Almighty Father, Son and Holy Ghost,
Eternal, ever-blessed, gracious God,
To me, the least of saints, to me allow
That I may keep a door in paradise;
That I may keep even the smallest door;
The furthest door, the darkest, the stiffest door,
If so it be but in thine house, O God!
If so it be that I can see thy glory,
Even afar and hear thy voice, O God!
And know that I am with thee, O God. Amen.

Is this what we desire?

For your journal…

1. What does the New Testament mean by suggesting that we look for 'the city that is to come' (Heb. 13:14)? In what ways are you looking for this city?

2. How can you show that you are thankful to God for the diversity of his people? Think about what the psalmist has been saying, especially in verse 4.

3. What specific things can you pray for that will bring 'peace' into God's church? Think about what the psalm says in verse 6.

Psalm 123

A Song of Ascents

1 To you I lift up my eyes,
    O you who are enthroned in the heavens!
2 Behold, as the eyes of servants
    look to the hand of their master,
as the eyes of a maidservant
    to the hand of her mistress,
so our eyes look to the LORD our God,
    till he has mercy upon us.

3 Have mercy upon us, O LORD, have mercy upon us,
    for we have had more than enough of contempt.
4 Our soul has had more than enough
    of the scorn of those who are at ease,
    of the contempt of the proud.

Day 4

Eyes right

> ➤ *Begin by reading Psalm 123.*
> ➤ *Pray about what you have read.*
> ➤ *Make notes on what you think God is teaching you.*
> ➤ *Read the chapter.*
> ➤ *Answer the questions in the section 'For your journal'.*

Psalm 123

Purblindness is a disease of the eye that affects vision: it causes short-sightedness. Things at a distance appear blurred and indistinct, whilst things close up are clearly visible. Without correcting lenses, purblindness is dangerous.

Let us fix our eyes on Jesus, the author of Hebrews exhorts (cf. Heb. 12:2), and this psalm does precisely the same. The problem it relates is one that is fairly common. It is spiritual purblindess, by which Christians fail to keep Jesus at the centre of their vision and stray away from the path he intends them to walk.

The psalmist, having finally arrived in Jerusalem and seen the greatness of the city (Ps. 122), is now brought down to earth with a bump! 'Our soul has had more than enough of the scorn of those who are at ease, of the contempt of the proud' (Ps. 123:4). Nothing reminds us of life in this world more than ridicule. To be mocked for our faith is something many have had to endure, and it is a reminder that life between the two comings of Jesus is marked, as Calvin so frequently said, by cross-bearing and self-denial. Not only that, but one gets the impression that the psalmist has reached the end of his tether! 'Have mercy upon us, O LORD, have mercy upon us, for we have had more than enough of contempt' (Ps. 123:3). It seems strange, doesn't it, that no sooner has the psalmist made it to Jerusalem, than he begins to complain. Things must have been difficult indeed! The inclusion of this complaint in this set of psalms is a reminder that opposition is a feature of the life of faith.

What does he do on remembering his ordeal? It is the well-worn route of prayer:

> Have we trials and temptations?
> Is there trouble anywhere?
> We should never be discouraged;
> Take it to the Lord in prayer.
>
> Joseph Scriven
> 1820-1886

'Prayer is the language of a man burdened with a sense of need,' wrote E. M. Bounds. Another more precise and theological definition of prayer is that of the *Shorter Catechism*:

> Prayer is an offering up of our desires unto God for things agreeable to his will, in the name of Christ, with confession of our sins, and thankful acknowledgement of his mercies.[1]

And here is another one: 'To you I lift up my eyes...' (Ps. 123:1). What simple eloquence these words convey! They are a glance in the direction of God, a look of faith at the Sovereign Lord. The Scottish Moravian hymn-writer captured the idea well in what is one of the best hymns of prayer:

Prayer is the soul's sincere desire,
Uttered or unexpressed,
The motion of a hidden fire
That trembles in the breast.

Prayer is the burden of a sigh,
The falling of a tear;
The upward glancing of an eye
When none but God is near.

James Montgomery
1771-1854

'The upward glancing of an eye...' — that is it exactly! It is the look of faith that casts an anchor upon the God of covenant promise. Parents can relate to this when they see a child looking longingly, with pleading eyes, without saying a word. Such glances are irresistible.

Prayer

Prayer focuses on God. This goes without saying, but it is interesting that Jesus taught his disciples to pray reminding them that, first of all, they must address their Father in heaven and hallow his name and desire that his kingdom and will be first in their lives (Matt. 6:9-13). In doing so, Jesus was reinforcing a lesson often ignored: we should think of God

before we think of *our*selves or *our* needs. God-centred living
will produce God-centred praying. Man-centred living will
produce man-centred praying. Just as trouble comes from
looking away from God, so trouble is alleviated by looking
to him. Just as the Lord's Prayer states, the psalmist reminds
himself that God is 'enthroned in the heavens' (123:1).

Two things are brought to our attention from this
reminder. One has to do with reverence. God is in heaven
and that will shape our prayer language. There can be no
place for flippancy and disrespect. What is embryonic here
is fully developed elsewhere. Think of the prayers of Ezra
or Daniel or Paul (Neh. 9:5-38; Ezra 9:6-15; Dan. 9:4-
19; Eph. 3:16-19). Such prayers, on examination, yield a
discipline whereby the thought of God's majesty is, as the
Puritans might have said, 'branched' — that is, yielding
several ways of thinking how precisely God's greatness is
manifested in various situations. As the seventeenth-century,
Northamptonshire Anglican, Thomas Fuller might have said,
such prayers can be like clothes that parents might buy their
children — several sizes too big in order that they might
grow into them. Here, in this psalm, the thought is in capsule
form: God's earthly throne might well be in Jerusalem, but it
was a reflection of where his true throne is — *heaven*! That
thought is designed to humble us. We are to remove from
our minds that which limits his greatness: 'Great is the LORD
and greatly to be praised in the city of our God! His holy
mountain...' (Ps. 48:1).

But this is not the main concern here. It is not *majesty*, but
might, that the psalmist has in mind. His 'throne' is in heaven.
To someone under threat, what is reassuring is not majesty so
much as power: God is *able* to deal with any foe. His power
knows no limits. There is nothing too hard for the Lord (see
Gen. 18:14). The thought that reassures the psalmist is that

God 'is able to do far more abundantly than all that we ask or think, according to the power at work within us' (Eph. 3:20). Such knowledge, 'that he is able to guard until that Day what has been entrusted to me', keeps us persevering (2 Tim. 1:12). There is no hostility that we face that we cannot bring to him and realize that, by comparison, it is nothing. His power overshadows the darkness. His sovereignty knows no limitation.

> And I am convinced that nothing can ever separate us from his love. Death cannot, and life cannot. The angels cannot, and the demons cannot. Our fears for today, our worries about tomorrow, and even the powers of hell cannot keep God's love away. Whether we are high above the sky or in the deepest ocean, nothing in all creation will be able to separate us from the love of God that is revealed in Christ Jesus our Lord
> (Rom. 8:38-39, New Living Translation).

> The avoidance of little evils, little sins, little inconsistencies, little weaknesses, little follies, little indiscretions and imprudences, little foibles, little indulgences of self and of the flesh, little acts of indolence or indecision or slovenliness or cowardice, little equivocations or aberrations from high integrity, little touches of shabbiness and meanness... little indifferences to the feelings or wishes of others, little outbreaks of temper, or crossness, or selfishness, or vanity — the avoidance of such *little* things as these goes far to make up at least the negative beauty of a holy life.
> Horatius Bonar, *God's Way of Holiness*[2]

Prayer is the expression of our helplessness. When the psalmist calls for 'mercy' (123:3), it seems as though he might well be saying, 'There is nothing I can do about this contempt I face. Lord, only you can help me face it.' In his weakness he calls on the Lord.

The psalm is beautifully illustrated by the actions of King Hezekiah upon receiving a threatening letter from the Assyrian king, Sennacherib. He took the letter into the temple and 'spread it before the LORD' (Isa. 37:14). It was as though Hezekiah was saying, 'I am powerless to face this enemy. It is you, not me, that he is actually threatening. Vindicate your name by coming to my defence.' It was a shrewd thing to do! God has a vested interest in defending his name and reputation, for his Word is on the line. He can no more deny his promise and covenant than he can deny himself: 'God is not mocked' (Gal. 6:7).

Helplessness is a mark of true spirituality. Its opposite is pride which, according to Augustine, is the very essence of sin. 'The greatest of men must turn beggars when they have to do with Christ,' said Matthew Henry.

Prayer appeals to the mercy of God. '...our eyes look to the LORD our God, till he has mercy upon us. Have mercy on us, O LORD, have mercy on us...' (Ps. 123:2-3). What the psalmist knows here is a truth that is characteristic of God: 'he delights in steadfast love' (Micah 7:18). He will never refuse those who ask him for mercy. God is not bound to exercise mercy. Mercy just wouldn't be mercy if it were obligatory.

The outstretched hand that contains nothing but a plea for mercy is idiomatic of the Christian life. Our days are filled with such prayers as these. There are a thousand issues in which we desire God to come and show mercy. We dare not ask God to give us what we deserve; we plead for that which we are not entitled to.

Hear gracious Lord, this voice that cries;
Have mercy, is my plea:
Let not Thine anger hide Thy face
Far, far away from me.
Thou only hast my helper been;
Forsake me not, I sigh;
Lift up Thy lovely face, and shine
Its beauty from on high.

Graham Harrison
1935-

The fight

Prayer is always a struggle. It is right here in the psalm; struggle
is the context of his praying. He seems to be saying that he
has been looking to the Lord, in the same way as a slave might
have done to his master, or a maid to her mistress (123:2);
but, so far, there has been no sign of any relief. He has been
casting his eye for the first sign of movement but all has been
still.

Even though the conflict is with the world, there is another
level at which this conflict engages, and that is with God
himself! So far God has been holding back, prolonging the trial
and thus stirring up the strife that he knows within his heart.

Have you known this? Sometimes, God refrains to answer
us quickly in order to write upon our hearts the lesson he
wishes us to learn. And what is that lesson? It is that prayer
is sometimes answered, as John Newton might have said, 'by
crosses'. God continues to make us stretch in order for us to
reach the heights of what true faith (and prayer) is: *trust* in
God alone!

Spiritual growth is hardly ever a uniform process. We grow, like children often do, in bursts of extension that have others saying, 'Look at how much you have grown!' Harsh trials can often cause that growth to accelerate in the same way that darkness can make vegetation sprout. There are seasons when we blossom. In Mississippi, where I now live, tulip and daffodil bulbs must first be placed in the refrigerator for several weeks to 'hoodwink' them into thinking that the Mississippi winter has come and gone! Just as certain bulbs will not grow unless they first feel the coldness of the frost, so Christians fail to grow unless they first experience trials.

Sometimes, the trial is prayer itself. Perseverance is difficult when answers do not seem to be forthcoming. These trials, too, as Jesus' parable of the friend at midnight relates, are meant to incite a persistence in our asking (Luke 11:2-8). We are, to cite one translation, to be 'shameless' in our persistence. 'Ask, and it will be given to you; seek, and you will find; knock, and it will be opened to you. For everyone who asks receives, and the one who seeks finds, and to the one who knocks it will be opened' (Luke 11:9-10).

There is a timetable to the providence of God that we need to discover. A believer looks to God, '*till* he has mercy upon us' (123:2, emphasis mine). Prayer recognizes this timetable and submits to it. There is a 'if it be your will' which prayer utters at every point. This should not be thought *immature*, as though mature prayers express things in ways which are more confident of the outcome. There is a discipline *in* prayer as much as there is a discipline *of* prayer. The difference between confidence and presumption in prayer is knowing what God has and has not promised to give. Prayer will only ask for that which God has pledged.

Waiting patiently on God's timing can be very difficult, of course. Such delays (and they are only delays from our perspective, not from God's) keep us on our toes (or better, on our knees!). They ensure that our faith is nourished rather than lulled into sleep. Abstinence creates an appetite. Growing in grace involves submission to God at every level and lessons learned here will repay dividends.

> Teach me Thy way, O Lord,
> Teach me Thy way!
> Thy gracious aid afford,
> Teach me Thy way!
> Help me to walk aright,
> More by faith, less by sight;
> Lead me with heavenly light;
> Teach me Thy way!

> Benjamin Mansell Ramsey
> 1849-1923

No wonder Robert Murray M'Cheyne could say, 'What a man is alone on his knees before God, that he is, and no more.' On that basis, what are we?

For your journal...

1. Write down two things that you can do to improve your prayer life.

2. Think of how you could take this psalm and turn it into a prayer of your own. What form would that prayer take?

3. What reasons can you give which may be causing you to struggle in prayer?

4. 'Waiting patiently on God's timing can be very difficult...' How will you improve your ability to wait on God's leading?

Psalm 124

A Song of Ascents. Of David.

1   *If it had not been the* LORD *who was on our side —*
    let Israel now say —
2   *if it had not been the* LORD *who was on our side*
    when people rose up against us,
3   *then they would have swallowed us up alive,*
    when their anger was kindled against us;
4   *then the flood would have swept us away,*
    the torrent would have gone over us;
5   *then over us would have gone*
    the raging waters.

6   *Blessed be the* LORD,
    who has not given us
    as prey to their teeth!
7   *We have escaped like a bird*
    from the snare of the fowlers;
  the snare is broken,
    and we have escaped!

8   *Our help is in the name of the* LORD,
    who made heaven and earth.

Day 5

If God be for us...

> ➢ *Begin by reading Psalm 124.*
> ➢ *Pray about what you have read.*
> ➢ *Make notes on what you think God is teaching you.*
> ➢ *Read the chapter.*
> ➢ *Answer the questions in the section 'For your journal'.*

Psalm 124

Imagine! It is the title of a well-known song by John Lennon. But, just imagine for a moment what life would be like apart from God's intervention. Imagine what it would be like if you were not a Christian. Imagine what might happen to you if God did not providentially prevent it. Imagine where we might be, what we might do, what others might do to us.

Psalm 124 is doing just that. It is imagining what might have happened had the Lord not intervened in the way that he did. The psalmist is asking for deliverance from an enemy, but in doing so, he recognizes that there are countless ways in which God has already protected him.

The climactic words that end the psalm have often been cited as a Call to Worship in Reformed liturgies, particularly by the French Protestants:

Our help is in the name of the LORD,
    who made heaven and earth

(Ps. 124:8).

The psalm itself forms something of a sandwich in which the outer layers (vv. 1-2 and 8) say the same thing, only from a negative and positive point of view, whilst the centre of the psalm (vv. 3-7) gives us four examples of deliverance.

Let's pretend

The psalm begins by asking the question, 'What if...?' 'If it had not been the LORD who was on our side...' (124:1).

- What if God hadn't stepped in the way he did?
- What if we had been left to our devices?
- What if providence had unfolded in some other way?

There are a million such questions. Consider the possible scenarios we might find ourselves in had history followed a different course, had God not ordered the direction of our lives the way he did. It is the observation, on the one hand, that our lives are ordered and governed by a sovereign providence. God's hand is on the tiller. The Creator continues to exercise a power in the world ensuring that all things take place according to a divine plan and purpose. Nothing happens by blind chance; even the falling of dice is by his decree. 'The lot is cast into the lap, but its every decision is from the LORD' (Prov. 16:33). When Ahab was fatally wounded by an arrow shot into the air at random in the course of battle, his ensuing death was in accord with the prophecy of Micaiah (2 Chr. 18:33). Joseph could say about his brothers' evil intent to kill him, 'As for you, you meant evil against me, but God meant it for good' (Gen. 50:20). God's hand may be hidden, but his rule is absolute. There is nothing that falls outside of his decree and personal involvement. He 'works all things according to the counsel of his will' (Eph. 1:11).

No one saw this truth clearer than Calvin in the course of the history of the Reformation. Writing in the *Institutes*, and alluding to the trials that Christians often face in this life, he has this to say:

> When dense clouds darken the sky, and a violent tempest arises, because a gloomy mist is cast over our eyes, thunder strikes our ears and all our senses are benumbed with fright, everything seems to us to be confused and mixed up; but all the while a constant quiet and serenity ever remain in heaven. So must we infer that, while the disturbances in the world deprive us of judgement, God out of the pure light of his justice and wisdom tempers and directs these very movements in the best-conceived order to a right end.[1]

Some think that the background to Psalm 124 lies in the account of David's coronation at Hebron, recorded in 2 Samuel 5. Following this ceremony, Jerusalem is taken from the Jebusites and in response to this, the Philistines come against David and his men in 'full force' (2 Sam. 5:17, NIV). The Philistines are conquered in a great battle at Perazim. They try again at the Valley of Rephaim and again, they are routed: 'And David did as the LORD commanded him, and struck down the Philistines from Geba to Gezer' (5:25).

Was this the victory signalled by our psalm? Perhaps it was. But, the beauty of the Psalms is that we don't know the exact context in which they were written, and that is so, because we are meant to place them in our own context. They are meant as expressions of faith *for us* in *our* struggles, and in *our* victories (and losses!). The scenario of verse 2, 'when people rose up against us', is one that is all too easily applied to our own situation. In our losses and crosses, we know all too well what Shakespeare called 'the slings and arrows of outrageous fortune'. But we also know that nothing happens without God willing it to happen; willing it to happen in the way that it did; willing it to happen *beforehand*.

> Deep in unfathomable mines
> Of never-failing skill,
> He treasures up his bright designs,
> And works his sovereign will.

William Cowper
1731-1800

Covenant mercies

Not only is this an assertion of a belief in providence in general, it is a testimony to Israel's covenant relationship with God in particular. The Lord was 'on our side' (124:1), the psalmist says with confidence. As though this is too good to be true, David (who is the author in this case) repeats it in verse 2 encouraging 'all Israel' to say it with him: 'If it had not been the LORD who was on our side — let Israel now say — if it had not been the LORD who was on our side when people rose up against us...' (124:1-2).

The victory had been God's doing. If the background here is the battle against the Philistines, then David and his men showed great ingenuity by attacking them from behind (2 Sam. 5:23). The strategy, however, was God-given and David simply did 'as the LORD commanded him' (5:25). He could take no credit, but could only ascribe the victory to God.

This had been the promise given to Israel on the plains of Moab as they contemplated the taking of Canaan: 'for the LORD your God is he who goes with you to fight for you against your enemies, to give you the victory' (Deut. 20:4). It was Jephthah's testimony in his victory over the Ammonites: 'the LORD gave them into my hand' (Judg. 12:3), just as Samson did in his battle with the Philistines (Judg. 15:18). 'Great salvation he brings to his king' was the promise God gave to David (2 Sam. 22:51) — something which David and others evidently recalled with gratitude as they penned their psalms while repeating and recalling the promise (compare Pss 18:50; 21:1, 5; 44:4; 108:13; 144:10).

> The truth is, I haven't any language weak enough to depict the weakness of my spiritual life. If I weakened it enough it would cease to be language at all. As when you try to turn the gas-ring a little lower still, and it merely goes out.
>
> C. S. Lewis, *Letters to Malcolm: Chiefly on Prayer* [2]

Whenever we realize that we are God's people, and that he fights 'for us', there comes an appreciation that all of our lives are held in his hands. This appreciation causes Paul to exclaim, 'If God is for us, who can be against us?' (Rom. 8:31). Paul seems to be proclaiming the truth of God's covenant commitment by citing from another psalm:

Be gracious to me, O God, for man tramples on me;
    all day long an attacker oppresses me;
my enemies trample on me all day long,
    for many attack me proudly.
When I am afraid,
    I put my trust in you.
In God, whose word I praise,
    in God I trust; I shall not be afraid.
    What can flesh do to me?
All day long they injure my cause;
    all their thoughts are against me for evil.
They stir up strife, they lurk;
    they watch my steps,
    as they have waited for my life.
For their crime will they escape?
    In wrath cast down the peoples, O God!

You have kept count of my tossings;
    put my tears in your bottle.
    Are they not in your book?
Then my enemies will turn back
    in the day when I call.
    This I know, that *God is for me.*
In God, whose word I praise,
    in the LORD, whose word I praise,
in God I trust; I shall not be afraid.
    What can man do to me?

I must perform my vows to you, O God;
    I will render thank offerings to you.
For you have delivered my soul from death,
    yes, my feet from falling,

>that I may walk before God
>   in the light of life

(Ps. 56, emphasis mine).

'*God is for me.*' These words bring to light what is at the heart of our relationship with God: he is committed to us. From the very start it has been so. The successive covenants which he made with Abraham, Moses and David have all been about this: he wants to form a love-relationship with us. And when this is so, we have no cause to be afraid — of anything! 'For I am sure that neither death nor life, nor angels nor rulers, nor things present nor things to come, nor powers, nor height nor depth, nor anything else in all creation, will be able to separate us from the love of God in Christ Jesus our Lord' (Rom. 8:38-39).

The psalmist in Psalm 124 has grasped something very precious indeed! If God had not been on his side, there is no limit to the catastrophe Israel would have known. The psalm mentions four possibilities: an earthquake (124:3), a flood (124:4), a beast of prey (124:6), and a 'fowler's snare' (124:7). Each one vividly captures the impending disaster that awaits those on whose behalf the Lord does not fight.

We must hold on to the same truth. In Jesus Christ (and in him alone!) God is 'for us'. Apart from faith in his Son, he is implacably opposed to us.

The Lord of battles

Christopher Wordsworth (1807-1885), a relative of the famous poet of the nineteenth century, wrote a hymn which contains the following verse:

Who is this that comes in glory
With the trump of jubilee?
Lord of battles, God of armies,
He has gained the victory;
He who on the cross did suffer,
He who from the grave arose,
He has vanquished sin and Satan,
He by death has spoiled His foes.

The background to this hymn may well be the words of Isaiah 63, a chapter which is amongst the most shocking in the Bible! It begins with the words: 'Who is this who comes ... in crimsoned garments...?' (Isa. 63:1). It is a picture of the Anointed One coming in the consummation of things as a warrior whose garments are spattered with the blood of his victims: 'their lifeblood spattered on my garments, and stained all my apparel' (Isa. 63:3). The mighty warrior has come for judgement and execution.

This theme of the 'God of Battles' is the one we have seen here in Psalm 124. It is a theme that the Bible gives us in more than one location. Early on in Exodus we are told, 'the LORD is a man of war; the LORD is his name' (Exod. 15:3). Isaiah, earlier in his prophecy, had signalled his coming: 'The LORD goes out like a mighty man, like a man of war he stirs up his zeal; he cries out, he shouts aloud, he shows himself mighty against his foes' (Isa. 42:13; compare Jer. 14:9; 20:11; Zeph. 1:14). It is a theme which also runs through the New Testament. Jesus comes to wage war against hostile and evil powers. He comes as the Mighty Warrior to enter into conflict against the ancient foe. He has come to destroy Satan.

The reason the Son of God appeared was to destroy the works of the devil

(1 John 3:8).

He disarmed the rulers and authorities and put them to open shame, by triumphing over them in him

(Col. 2:15).

Since therefore the children share in flesh and blood, he himself likewise partook of the same things, that through death he might destroy the one who has the power of death, that is, the devil, and deliver all those who through fear of death were subject to lifelong slavery

(Heb. 2:14-15).

What these verses allude to is a battle which is first brought to the surface in Genesis 3:15, the so-called *protoevangelium*, or first gospel-promise. The promise is given that from the seed of the woman (Eve) would come one who would crush the head of Satan, even though Satan would manage to bruise his heel in the process. The prince of death is defeated by Christ's substitutionary and propitiatory death on behalf of sinners. 'Paul with good reason, therefore,' writes Calvin, 'magnificently proclaims the triumph that Christ obtained for himself on the cross, as if the cross, which was full of shame, had been changed into a triumphal chariot!'[3] As Jesus himself had said, the house of the 'strong man' has been plundered (Matt. 12:29; Mark 3:27; Luke 11:21).

It is to this triumph of God that culminates in the victory achieved at the cross that this psalm ultimately speaks. Through the shout of triumph, 'It is finished' (John 19:30), Jesus has achieved the ultimate deliverance that enables us to say, 'If God is for us, who can be against us?' (Rom. 8:31). This is the assurance that keeps us persevering.

'Blessed be the LORD ... we have escaped!'

In 1582, an imprisoned minister, John Durie, was set free in Edinburgh and he discovered as he walked into the city that he was met by two hundred of his friends. The number is said to have increased to two thousand, who began to sing as they walked down High Street the words of this psalm, 'Now Israel may say...' It is said that one of his persecutors was more alarmed by this than by anything he had seen in Scotland.

For your journal...

1. Take a few moments to reflect on where you might be today *if* God had not intervened in your life. Be sure to thank him that he did intervene!

2. Meditate on God's 'warrior' qualities. Do you need to adjust your view of God as a consequence of what the Bible teaches and what this psalm teaches us?

3. Think about how God has shown himself 'on your side' in your recent experience. As you think about this, ask yourself why you think that these things prove that God is 'on your side'.

4. 'Praise the Lord' occurs over seven thousand times in the Bible! How does this statistic affect you?

Psalm 125

A Song of Ascents

1 *Those who trust in the LORD are like Mount Zion,*
        which cannot be moved, but abides for ever.
2 *As the mountains surround Jerusalem,*
        so the LORD surrounds his people,
        from this time forth and for evermore.
3 *For the sceptre of wickedness shall not rest*
        on the land allotted to the righteous,
     lest the righteous stretch out
        their hands to do wrong.
4 *Do good, O LORD, to those who are good,*
        and to those who are upright in their hearts!
5 *But those who turn aside to their crooked ways*
        the LORD will lead away with evildoers!
        Peace be upon Israel!

Day 6

Surrounded

> ➤ *Begin by reading Psalm 125.*
> ➤ *Pray about what you have read.*
> ➤ *Make notes on what you think God is teaching you.*
> ➤ *Read the chapter.*
> ➤ *Answer the questions in the section 'For your journal'.*

Psalm 125

'Behold, the Lord GOD comes with might ... He will tend his flock like a shepherd; he will gather the lambs in his arms; he will carry them in his bosom, and gently lead those that are with young' (Isa. 40:10-11).

So spoke Isaiah the prophet in the eighth century B.C., and in so doing uttered one of the most reassuring themes the Bible unfolds: that God is our sovereign protector.

Augustus Toplady (1740-1778), the hymn-writer, put it succinctly in these words:

A sovereign protector I have,
Unseen, yet for ever at hand;
Unchangeably faithful to save;
Almighty to rule and command.
He smiles, and my comforts abound;
His grace as the dew shall descend,
And walls of salvation surround
The soul He delights to defend.

This is the theme of Psalm 125. The context is a familiar one. The psalmist is troubled by the fact that wickedness is all around him. His enemies appear to occupy areas which rightfully belong to the Lord's people (125:3). Perhaps this indicates that this psalm comes from a later period, possibly during the time of the Babylonian exile. The psalmist is trying to sing the Lord's song in a strange land knowing that 'foreigners' are occupying his own. In the space of just five verses, we hear the refrain of 'wickedness', 'wrong', 'crooked ways' and 'evildoers', which signal how preoccupied he is with the trouble he faces. But this is not one of those psalms that 'sings the blues'. There is no hint here, as elsewhere, of despair and gloom at the prospect of the advances of evil (cf. Pss 13, 42, 43, 73, 102). This is not a psalm in which there is the suspicion of abandonment and desertion by God. On the contrary, the psalmist is rejoicing in the certainty of divine protection. He feels upheld and sustained.

What this psalm is saying is something like this: 'This is where I, the Lord, have placed my feet, now, walk in my footsteps. Follow me in your life's journey and discover these truths about God that can sustain you and keep you. The darkness may be surrounding you, but you are to be assured, as a child of God, that greater realities abound. I, the Lord, am round about you. My arms enfold you.'

Realism and the struggle of faith

There exists a great deal of confusion about the nature of the Christian life. Unreality about suffering and trials make some presentations of kingdom life bizarre and destined for psychological breakdown. A belief that God intends no suffering for his children warps the perspective of some into one of two directions: some, fancying optimistic expectations of sanctification, expect levels of living that are above the common fray. Like aircraft that ascend above the clouds, so Christians can live in such dizzy heights that troubles do not (should not) affect them any more. Those who discover that trials very much do affect them still, are further troubled. Refusing to acknowledge an unrealistic theology, they either pretend the problem doesn't exist, or else they fall victim to the pressure and become emotional wrecks. Others draw the logical conclusion of their position, that God intends no suffering for his children, and suggest that all suffering is demonic. Turning God into a figure of extraordinary impotence and passivity, suffering is described as the activity of Satan. To cite a modern form of this view: when bad things happen to good people, God has nothing to do with it.

The psalms come to us like a breath of fresh air in the musty confines that these perspectives relate. They are thoroughly realistic in their portrayal of life. No one can read them without being impressed by the audacious way in which they relate frustration and fear, doubt and despair. Calvin put it this way:

> [The psalmists] lay open their inmost thoughts and affections, call, or rather draw, each of us to the examination of himself in particular, in order that none of the many infirmities to which we are subject, and of the many vices with which we abound, may remain concealed.[1]

Imagine the psalmist in Jerusalem surrounded by the great sites and smells of the city and temple. And what is he doing? What thoughts come into his mind? His troubles! It is one of the reasons we find the Psalms so appealing, isn't it? Because, there is no attempt to suggest some unrealistic spirituality to which we cannot relate. There is an honesty here that is breathtaking and welcome. This is what we have known, too. In the midst of a worship service, we have found our minds wandering and focusing on issues that trouble us. In the very act of prayer we have discovered that for some time we have been preoccupied by something that concerns us and we have stopped talking to talk!

We find ourselves in this world, in this *fallen* world in which Satan reigns to some degree, where he is 'the prince of the power of the air' (Eph. 2:2). As I was writing these lines, news came to me of two ministers with whom I briefly shared some classes whilst at seminary. Then I heard that one had lost both of his teenage children in an accident, and another had a fourteen-year-old son who shot himself accidentally and is cerebrally dead. Theologies that don't take into account these possibilities and offer words of counsel and support are worthless. Worse than that, they are demonic! Like Satan who lies, these theologies distort and rob at the point of greatest need. This, the Psalms never do. The very reality of the warfare in which the believer finds himself is a worldview with which the Psalms readily associate.

'In the world you will have tribulation' (John 16:33).

Whatever kind of tribulation presses upon us, we must ever look to this end: to accustom ourselves to contempt for the present life and to be aroused thereby to meditate upon the future life. For since God knows best how much we are inclined by nature to a brutish love of this world, he uses the fittest means to draw us back and to shake off our sluggishness, lest we cleave too tenaciously to that love. There is not one of us, indeed, who does not wish to seem throughout his life to aspire and strive after heavenly immortality.

John Calvin, Institutes of the Christian Religion[2]

The recourse of prayer

It bears repeating because it is so true:

> Have we trials and temptations?
> Is there trouble anywhere?
> We should never be discouraged,
> Take it to the Lord in prayer.

Joseph Scriven
1820-1886

It is important for us to catch what the psalmist is doing as he moves from one verse to another in this psalm:

> For the sceptre of wickedness shall not rest
>   on the land allotted to the righteous,
> lest the righteous stretch out
>   their hands to do wrong.
> Do good, O LORD, to those who are good,
>   and to those who are upright in their hearts!
> (Ps. 125:3-4).

Verse 3 is difficult, but essentially what it is saying is this: the land of Israel was under occupation by foreign armies (the

Assyrians, or possibly the Babylonians). But they were not to occupy 'the land' for ever. Why not? Because God had made certain promises concerning 'the land' and its inhabitants. 'The land' was part of the promise given to Abraham (Gen. 17:8). Even though God had threatened exile from 'the land' on account of disobedience on the part of Israel, that exile was limited in its duration. As Daniel was to discover, reading from Jeremiah 29:10, that time was to be seventy years (Dan. 9:2). It is important, therefore, that following the statement of the promise in verse 3, there is a prayer in verse 4 calling for its fulfilment. Just as Daniel turned this promise into the great prayer of Daniel 9, so the psalmist does the same here.

Promises never lead to fatalism in the Bible — never! The Bible writers did not draw the conclusion that because God has given his word about something, and because God's purposes can never be frustrated, they had therefore nothing to do but to watch him fulfil them. That is fatalism, not Christianity! Bible writers turned promises into prayers. They understood that the way God fulfils his promises is in answer to our praying. He will be asked before he delivers. He ordains the means as well as the end.

There is a link here between meditation and prayer. As the psalmist thinks about God and his Word, so he turns his thoughts and discoveries into prayer. The promises of God meditated upon, form the fuel that fires his intercessions. It is always a good way to pray. 'Turn the Bible into prayer,' said Robert Murray M'Cheyne. 'God's promises are the cork to keep faith from sinking in prayer,' said Thomas Watson. 'Prayer', wrote John Bunyan on a more formal level, 'is a sincere, sensible affectionate pouring out of the soul to God, through Christ, in the strength and assistance of the Spirit, for such things as God has promised.'[3]

What exactly does he pray for? What is prayed for in verse 4 seems to be asserted in verse 5, as though the psalmist received an immediate assurance that he had been heard! Praying that God would bless the upright in heart (125:4) leads the psalmist to assert that '...those who turn aside to their crooked ways the LORD will lead away with evildoers!' (125:5).

There is a recognition here that God will act in conformity to a certain rule, or standard. The assertion that follows the prayer is made not about the righteous, but about the wicked. This is not one of those dark prayers that sometimes finds its way into the Psalms, and with which certain people have trouble, especially when they don't take seriously what God says about his holiness and what that will mean for the unrepentant. No, this is an assertion based upon the fact that God always acts this way. God's dealings with the wicked are never erratic, or fitful; there is a predictability about the way God acts, and this is because he always acts according to his Word, his covenant. That's what makes the God of Israel different from all the gods of the nations around: the covenant LORD of Israel can be trusted to do as he has promised.

Recently, a criticism has emerged from those who desire to see in God an 'openness' about the future. They suggest that God is subject to change in the same way that we are. 'After all,' they say, 'doesn't the Bible speak of God "repenting"?' Indeed, it does! But rather than suggest, as the church has been saying for centuries, and as Calvin eloquently said in the sixteenth century, that these are 'anthropomorphisms' — 'baby talk', if you like, designed to speak down to our level — critics have said this unnecessarily hems God in. Indeed it does! And what blessings accrue as a result of it; not least of which is that we know where we are with God. We do not find ourselves thinking that God acts this way today and another way tomorrow. In all his dealings with us there is a conformity to principle, to revealed law, to biblical norm that makes our relationship with him testable and safe. The psalmist knew what the end of the wicked was, because God had spoken it. That was the end of the matter. He was not to discover that God had changed his mind about something he had revealed centuries earlier. That gives us courage to rest in his promises and take him at his word. And that, more than anything else, is the best comfort of all.

But what is that promise as it relates to the believer? Of what can I be assured?

Encircled by love

The opening verses of the psalm use a graphic picture of what it means to trust in the Lord and his promises.

> As the mountains surround Jerusalem,
>   so the LORD surrounds his people,
>   from this time forth and for evermore
>
> (Ps. 125:2).

Topographically, Jerusalem — then as now — is surrounded by a range of mountains. Zion, on which the city is built, is a mountain amongst other mountains. The picture is one of encirclement and protection. And this is said to picture the relationship God has to his people. He encircles and protects them.

Deuteronomy pictures God as bearing his arms *underneath*, as it were, ready to catch someone who trips and falls, 'The eternal God is your dwelling place, and underneath are the everlasting arms' (Deut. 33:27). Isaiah pictures God as Shepherd, gently enfolding his arms around a lamb and carrying it home, 'He will tend his flock like a shepherd; he will gather the lambs in his arms; he will carry them in his bosom, and gently lead those that are with young' (Isa. 40:11). These pictures convey the notion that God says of those he carries, 'These are mine! I love them!' It belongs to the same order of thought as the idea expressed by Jesus when he described himself as a hen eagerly wanting her chicks to come and take refuge under her wings (Matt. 23:37; Luke 13:34). This is what God is essentially like, Jesus is saying.

'...for evermore' (125:2).

The promise never ends.

> O Love, that wilt not let me go,
> I rest my weary soul in Thee!

> George Matheson
> 1842-1906

That is why the psalm ends with a benediction: 'Peace be upon Israel!' (Ps. 125:5). Whatever may be happening around us, we are never outside of God's protection — never! We are garrisoned by this peace. 'And the peace of God, which surpasses all understanding, will guard your hearts and your minds in Christ Jesus' (Phil. 4:7).

In the wake of the financial ruin following the great fires of Chicago in 1873, Horatio Spafford sent his wife and daughters to England only to learn that his daughters had drowned in an accidental collision at sea. Making the same voyage and halting at the spot where they perished he wrote the words that express with moving simplicity and faith, what this psalm is saying:

When peace like a river, attendeth my way,
When sorrows like sea billows roll;
Whatever my lot, thou hast taught me to say,
'It is well, it is well with my soul.'

Horatio Spafford
1828-1888

It is the reassurance that every Christian may know.

God keeps us safe no matter what happens!

For your journal...

1. As you think about yourself, or your family, or your friends, what struggles of faith come to mind?

2. What promises of the Bible are especially comforting to you? Write two of them down that are particularly precious to you. Is there one other promise that you have found in the reading today that you could add to your favourite promises?

3. The fact that the psalm ends with 'Israel' is a reminder of the corporate dimension of our faith. Make a list of people that you want to pray for today.

4. Did you learn something in particular from this psalm? What was it?

Psalm 126

A Song of Ascents

1 When the LORD restored the fortunes of Zion,
    we were like those who dream.
2 Then our mouth was filled with laughter,
    and our tongue with shouts of joy;
then they said among the nations,
    'The LORD has done great things for them.'
3 The LORD has done great things for us;
    we are glad.

4 Restore our fortunes, O LORD,
    like streams in the Negeb!
5 Those who sow in tears
    shall reap with shouts of joy!
6 He who goes out weeping,
    bearing the seed for sowing,
shall come home with shouts of joy,
    bringing his sheaves with him.

Day 7

Holy tears and holy laughter

> ➤ *Begin by reading Psalm 126.*
> ➤ *Pray about what you have read.*
> ➤ *Make notes on what you think God is teaching you.*
> ➤ *Read the chapter.*
> ➤ *Answer the questions in the section 'For your journal'.*

Psalm 126

It sounds almost trite to say it, but the Lord's people are still *in this world*. 'Tears' are the order of the day (126:5).

It is interesting, as we take just a cursory look at this psalm, that it begins with tears and ends with laughter. It signals to us one of the reasons why it is that so many of us find this psalm resonating with our own personal experience of life in this world. We, too, find life mixed with tears and laughter.

This psalm is set in a definite context. Lying behind the psalm is the experience of exile which must have been traumatic in a way that is hard for us even to imagine and contemplate. And yet, there is about this psalm something very personal with which we immediately identify. Each one of us can testify to knowing God's deliverances in such a way that when they come, we say to ourselves, 'We were like those who dream' (126:1). So great and overwhelming are the mighty works of God's deliverances that we can scarcely take them in!

The background to this psalm undoubtedly belongs to that period of history that is recorded for us in the books of Ezra and Nehemiah. After seventy years of captivity in Babylon, God brought his people back again to the land of promise. Most of those who came back had never known anything else except life in Babylon. There were exceptions — men like Daniel, for example, people now in their eighties and nineties who would have been transported as teenagers to Babylon. They were now to return to a land that had only been kept alive in the stories that had been told to them. They had never known, or at best could only dimly remember, what it was to walk in the regions of Upper Galilee, or the plains of central Palestine, or, more importantly, the hills of Mount Zion. They had only the faintest knowledge of what Jerusalem was like. They knew nothing of the temple and its worship; the sacrifices and feasts that had marked out their calendar had been missing from their worship in Babylon. Can you imagine the sense of joy as they return to Canaan and the ruined walls of the city and the temple?

The psalm divides into three sections: a song, a prayer and a promise. The song is in verses 1-3, the prayer is found in verse 4 and the promise concludes the psalm in verses 5-6.

It begins with a song — a song of deliverance. It is a cameo portrait of the story of the church in the Old Testament. There is captivity and there is restoration or deliverance, and this repeats itself. There is Egypt and there is Canaan. There is Babylon and there is the restoration that followed it. And, as we have suggested, what lies behind this psalm is that deportation that took place in 586 B.C., when the Lord raised up Nebuchadnezzar to chasten his people, and some two generations later raised up Darius to restore them again. There was the decree of the King of Babylon to destroy the temple and there was the decree of the King of Persia to rebuild it. And in many ways, it is the entire story of the Old Testament.

It is important for us to grasp the perspective on history that the psalmist adopts. It was *sacred* history; it was the Lord's doing. The psalmist is essentially saying, 'It is the LORD who has brought us back; and it is the LORD who has done great things' (126:1-3). Men may do their worst and they may do their best, but ultimately it is God who weaves history together. It is the perspective that history is *his* story. It is by his providence that God orders all the events and details of everything that happens to us, individually and collectively, for a divine purpose which we may or may not understand.

Most of our problems come from a failure to realize this fact. No matter what it is, or how great or evil a deed it may be, the unfolding of history takes place by the outworking of a sovereign hand on the controls.

Problems may vary, of course. Some are work related, some threaten health, and others involve communal relationships of marriage, home and family. Some are self-imposed, the results of pride, jealousy and frustration. And when deliverance comes to any of these situations it is as though we are dreaming.

Have you ever talked to someone who has been delivered from the threat of cancer, to a person who has lived through the fear of disease and death? It is like a dream, isn't it? You can hardly believe that it is real! There is a moment in Cecil B. DeMille's portrayal of the life of Moses in *The Ten Commandments* when he describes a figure who is anxious and troubled. When Moses commands the waters of the Red Sea to stand in a heap on either side so that the people can pass through, he has a little man say to his family as they are passing through the gap in the waters, 'Hurry, hurry!' He can hardly believe that it is true, or that it will last for much longer.

Actually, the psalm indicates a twofold reaction, the first by the people of God in which they are filled with songs and laughter, and are saying, 'The Lord has done this!', and the second, by the nations saying something similar (v. 2). One of the reasons that lay behind God sending the plagues on Egypt and on Pharaoh in particular, was that the Egyptians would say of the exodus of the Jews, 'God has done this!' (cf. Exod. 7:5).

There is a sense in which every Christian has known this deliverance. What else does it mean to be a Christian but that we have been delivered from the dark night of sin and brought into the liberty of an adopted condition as the children of God? And in that sense, each one of us ought to rejoice with joy unspeakable and full of glory.

Grace flooding the soul

Secondly, there is not only a song in this psalm; there is also a prayer. 'Restore our fortunes, O LORD, like streams in the Negeb!' (126:4). The Negeb was in the south, a dry and barren desert land that stretched from just below Jerusalem down to the regions of Beersheba. To this day, it is inhospitable terrain as anyone will know who has been to Israel and gone on the tourist routes down to the Dead Sea, the regions of Massada, and beyond.

What the psalmist is thinking about here is the reality of life as he had known it, perhaps, after returning from Babylon. Not everyone returned, of course. Some preferred to stay in

Babylon rather than risk a life of uncertain existence in Israel again. But those who did, as the first few chapters of Ezra tell us in detail, were faced with setbacks and hostility; the experience of joy and gladness was soon tinged with the bitterness of tears again (v. 5). There were disappointments, some of which were to come from the inconsistencies of the Lord's people. And what the psalmist does now in this prayer is to employ a graphic image known to many who had lived in these southern regions of Israel. The terrain, baked by the heat of the sun, had become hard. Without warning, whenever the rains fell in the northern slopes of the country, the water would come rushing down and fill the wadis of the Negeb very quickly. Flooding was a very real threat whenever the rains came. What the psalmist is praying for is just such a flood — a flood of the grace of God to come rushing down and sweep them off their feet.

> Lord, end my winter, and let my spring begin. I cannot with all my longing raise my soul out of her *death and dullness*, but all things are possible with thee. I need celestial influences, the clear shinings of thy love, the beams of thy grace, the light of thy countenance, these are the Pleades to me. I suffer much from sin and temptation, these are my wintry signs, my terrible Orion. Lord, work wonders in me, and for me.
>
> C. H. Spurgeon, *Morning and Evening*[1]

It is an understandable prayer, isn't it? It is the longing of our hearts as we think about the condition of the church today. We, too, long for the waters of revival to come down and sweep away the lethargy and despondency that so often grips the church of Jesus Christ. But the reality is that we live our lives in the sphere of difficulty. It is a time of leanness. It is a time of stress and pain. That's the reality of life, isn't it? That's where some of us are right now! *You* can relate to that. This is a picture of *you*, longing for the spiritual showers to fall and sweep down and flood *your* life again.

And the sentiment here is no different from that expressed in the Old Testament, and particularly in the prophets where God is said to come down, and return, and visit so that consciences are quickened, spirits enlivened, hearts encouraged, and faith revived (see Pss 44:23-26; 69:18; 80:14).

Is this your prayer?

Workshop downstairs, showroom upstairs!

There is also a promise in this psalm of great significance, that though we may find ourselves weeping, this is part of the process that leads to a harvest. Painful sowing leads to fruitful reaping — it is the rule of the kingdom of God. 'Unless a grain of wheat falls into the earth and dies...,' Jesus said that there will be no harvest (John 12:24). There must be a dying before life can emerge. The law of harvest dictates that there can be no fruitful gathering unless a death has first taken place. Pain and suffering is the conduit through which true life emerges and blossoms. Whatever the difficulties may appear to be, God will ensure the final outcome of life. He will meticulously add all the finishing touches to the canvas.

You may not be able to put all the pieces together; the work appears incomplete, half done, but the covenant of grace assures us and the finished work of Christ assures us too, and the continual intercession of Christ still further assures us that he will complete what he has started. There will be a day of harvest. Right now you may be called upon to suffer; it may be that for now, tears are more in abundance than anything else. This sounds depressing, doesn't it? But, be patient, for the Master hasn't finished his work yet. This is but the workshop that you see now; the showroom is upstairs.

What we have here is the counterpart to what Paul says so eloquently in Romans 8, that if we suffer with him (Christ), we shall be glorified with him. This is a salutary reminder that suffering is so much a part of the experience of the church in this time between the two advents of Jesus. There *is* a harvest coming, a harvest so great that it is difficult to conceive!

Our sowing may involve tears, but God knows our tears. Psalm 56:8 tells us that he records them on a scroll and keeps them as a record. Isn't that extraordinary? We have a Saviour who has shed tears at the grave of a dear friend and who now knows how to sympathize with those that fall down our cheeks. One moment in heaven will wipe away every tear! Then, the purposes of God will have ripened and the plan of God will have been executed and not one of his plans will have gone astray.

Isn't that wonderful?

Lay hold of that promise and pray that something of it might come flooding into your soul as you mediate upon it.

The lesson of this psalm is to 'keep on keeping on'. It is to take the next step, and then the next, and then the next. The fruit may not be immediate. But, be faithful... never give up.

For your journal...

1. The psalm today has been focusing upon the history of Israel. Think about your own past and reflect upon the providences of God that have worked to bring you to where you are today.

2. How sincere are you in wanting the floods of God's grace to pour into your soul? What aspects of your life might change as a result?

3. Why should pain lead to glory? Is this always true? Reflect what you might be learning from pain in your life.

Psalm 127

A Song of Ascents. Of Solomon.

1   Unless the LORD builds the house,
        those who build it labour in vain.
    Unless the LORD watches over the city,
        the watchman stays awake in vain.
2   It is in vain that you rise up early
        and go late to rest,
    eating the bread of anxious toil;
        for he gives to his beloved sleep.

3   Behold, children are a heritage from the LORD,
        the fruit of the womb a reward.
4   Like arrows in the hand of a warrior
        are the children of one's youth.
5   Blessed is the man
        who fills his quiver with them!
    He shall not be put to shame
        when he speaks with his enemies in the gate.

Day 8

Built to last

> ➤ *Begin by reading Psalm 127.*
> ➤ *Pray about what you have read.*
> ➤ *Make notes on what you think God is teaching you.*
> ➤ *Read the chapter.*
> ➤ *Answer the questions in the section 'For your journal'.*

Psalm 127

The opening words of this psalm in Latin are: *Nisi Dominus frustra*, and they are the basis for the motto of the city of Edinburgh, Scotland. They mean: 'Without the Lord it is vain', and they capture the main point of this psalm.

'I'm having trouble sleeping!' It is a common enough problem that afflicts us all at some time or another. Reasons vary; often complex psychological and physiological factors are at work, requiring accurate diagnosis and alleviation.

But sometimes, too, the causes are simple enough: worry, anxiety, distrust of God's providence, or care, or both. And that would seem to be what Solomon is getting at here in this psalm. It is a psalm that says, 'Don't worry!'

Don't you hate it when someone says that? You say to yourself, 'What does he know about my situation? I have things to worry about!' The world can sometimes be cruel and dismissive of the concerns that we have; the Bible is never that way. It never suggests that we live in denial of reality. Avoiding the issue which is causing us anxiety is never a road to peace. What the Bible does is to take the issue seriously, suggesting that we consider a wider worldview in which a sovereign, omnipotent God loves and cares for his people — a worldview in which God's providence orders everything. The problem is real enough, but God is bigger than the problem, and that fact gives Christians a certain perspective that others do not have.

Remember the words of Jesus: 'Therefore do not be anxious about tomorrow, for tomorrow will be anxious for itself. Sufficient for the day is its own trouble' (Matt. 6:34). Or, as a well-known hymn puts it:

All the way my Saviour leads me;
What have I to ask beside?
Can I doubt his tender mercy,
Who through life has been my guide?
Heavenly peace, divinest comfort,
Here by faith in Him to dwell
For I know, whate'er befall me
Jesus doeth all things well.[1]

Fanny Crosby
1823-1915

It is that confidence that saturates this psalm.

There are three areas of concern highlighted in this psalm: domestic, urban and familial. Our homes affect us deeply for this is where we live and spend our lives. The city is where we work and trade, and the threat of economic collapse and urban violence is all too real. Our families are what we live for — their well-being is uppermost on our list of priorities. The psalm touches every sphere of our lives; vocation, marriage, economic security — these are the areas that occupy us each day of our lives. The psalm could hardly be more relevant. It refers to everything that belongs to our personal, domestic and civil lives. If the Lord isn't at the centre of it, then it isn't worth anything at all. Its value is diminished, and we are left impoverished and broken as a result. It is just here that Abraham Kuyper's words seem appropriate: 'There isn't a square inch of this universe over which the Lord does not say, "Mine!"'

Personal prosperity. We can imagine the psalmist in Jerusalem turning his thoughts towards home! Perhaps he has expended a great deal of time and energy in obtaining for himself a good home. Perhaps he is proud of it, or even dissatisfied with it. And now that he is away from home he begins to think about it and comes to realize something of fundamental importance: 'Unless the LORD builds the house...' Stress counsellors tell us that next to divorce, moving is one of the greatest stress factors that we can experience.

It all too probable that what the psalmist is thinking about here is economic security. In an agrarian economy, fiscal security was notoriously uncertain. Disease, for example, could wipe out an entire family's fortune. Without social security or government intervention programmes, it was doubly important to seek the Lord's blessing on monetary matters. This, too, was an area where God was paramount.

Personal security. But there is a second area that the psalmist relates, one which also gives rise to worry and concern. It is what he refers to as the 'city'. Picture the watchman here, in the darkness trying to stay awake, but there is nothing he can do if he cannot see the enemy infiltrating. They may already be inside the Trojan horse. Imagine how people felt in some of those cities in Iraq, for example, when they thought that a 'stealth bomber', which is invisible to radar detection, was coming. Do you see what the psalmist is saying? With all our sophistication, we still need the Lord to guard the city.

Our anxiety over life and death issues is pointless because in the end we are not in control of them! We may think we are, because we are getting very clever and sophisticated in medical intervention, but without God's intervention, without the sovereign hand of God, we are without hope.

The city was a place of protection in primitive times. It is the place where country folk ran for shelter from an invading army. Today, it is more likely that the reverse is true. To avoid trouble, we tend to flee the city. Whether it is the threat of nuclear attack, or moral disintegration, the city is at the centre of the enemy's target. Our cities are the core of most of our social concerns. Pornography, drug abuse and crime... these are things we associate with the big city. Many social commentators of our time have viewed the city as the heart of our problem. Sin concentrates in cities. While the cities may have offered protection in Bible times, it was no less true then as it is now, they are centres of sin, and the psalmist is reflecting on the need for divine intervention to prevent the total collapse of his own society.

Personal relationships. We also worry about our children. Solomon may be thinking about his home — not so much the building, but what is inside it: his family! And he's saying something of profound significance; that unless we think of our families in terms of the Lord and his work, then all is in vain. This speaks to us at profoundly deep levels. We *do* worry about our families; we *do* worry about our children, what they are and what they will become. This is a major concern of any marriage that seeks to honour Christ. Churches, too, expend a great deal of energy on youth work and ensure that appropriate people are asked to minister to this age group. But this psalm is reminding us of something deeper still. Above everything else, our concern must be for God to work his grace and purpose out in our families. All we do in terms of providing for them, spending time with them, taking them to soccer and football and scouts and whatever else, doesn't amount to anything if we aren't ensuring that God is right in the middle of our families.

Whatever else may be concluded, it is clear that in the Old Testament there is a concern for the family in God's covenant dealings with his people. Every covenant in the Old Testament has the family as its basic structure.

The covenant with Adam has this structure, according to Paul's exegesis of Genesis 1 - 3 in Romans 5:12-21. The covenant curse that fell on Adam falls on all those who are in Adam — that is, on Adam and his seed. The family is included in the overall structure of the covenant.

The covenant with Noah was also made with his seed. This is implicit in Genesis 6:18 (but is made explicit in Genesis 9:8): 'But I will establish my covenant with you, and you shall come into the ark, you, your sons, your wife, and your sons' wives with you.'

The covenant with Abraham has the same features (Gen. 15:18; 17:1-4). The same is true of the covenant made with Moses, in which God remembers his covenant with Abraham, Isaac and Jacob (Exod. 2:24; compare 6:2,6 — that covenant is fulfilled in the contemporary Israelites and their families; compare Deut. 29:9-14). The same is true of the Davidic covenant (Ps. 89:3-4; compare 2 Sam. 22:51; 23:5).

It is interesting to see that Peter makes this very point on the Day of Pentecost, stating very clearly that the 'promise' of God is made 'for you and for your children...' (Acts 2:39). Clearly, God is concerned about the family.

Perhaps the worshipper here might have been looking at his family as he brought them to one of the great festivals in Jerusalem and he was thinking to himself: 'The most important thing for my family is for God to build it.' Can't you say 'Amen' to that?

Now we need to appreciate something that is a distinctive feature of the Old Testament and that is the picture drawn for us in the closing verses of this psalm, namely, of a man who has many sons, his quiver full; they are standing at the gate where his enemies are, and they are ensuring that justice is being done on behalf of their father. It is a beautiful picture that many of you can relate to as you think about the children you have. But the point is that this, too, is God's doing. The emphasis is upon the sovereignty of God in providence — in the home, in the city and in the family.

But if these are three areas that cause anxiety (and they are), note how the psalmist injects into this setting three great theological truths designed to underscore this very point: *God is sovereign and is to be trusted with everything that has to do with our lives.*

...growth in grace is always growth by grace and under grace, never beyond grace; and grace means God enriching sinners. That is who we are. We do not grow beyond grace. We never get to a point where we can cease to thank God for Calvary on a day-to-day basis, or to humble ourselves before him as hell-deserving sinners.

J. I. Packer, *Knowing Christianity*[2]

The God who sustains

God rules. God builds, he guards and he creates (vv. 1,3). God is in control. He hasn't lost any of his power or ability. His ability to do things is not diminished to any degree. God's will is supreme. It is inviolable and his decree is irresistible.

How did Paul find it within himself to say, as he did, to the Philippians, 'I have learned the secret of facing plenty and hunger, abundance and need' (Phil. 4:12). To be content literally means 'to be independent of my circumstances', to be at peace with myself, with my conscience, with the world, and with God. There are no qualifications, no set of contingencies that would make him think otherwise. It is what we see worked out in Acts 16 where Paul and Silas are in a Philippian jail at midnight — and what are they doing? They are singing psalms! Here is a man who knew what it was to receive thirty-nine lashes, to be shipwrecked, to be disinherited by his parents, to be the scorn of false prophets, and to know a thorn in the flesh that troubled him greatly; *yet he was content in those circumstances*!

There is only one explanation for this. It is the little statement in Philippians 4, found in the same context as that expression about contentment: 'The Lord is at hand' (Phil. 4:5). God is beside him! He is close to him, watching over his situation. Paul was constantly aware of and thinking about the presence of the Lord and what that implied.

God is taking care of me!

God is in complete control!

We are to take our stand on the principle, 'Your will be done.' That was the position that Jesus took, wasn't it? 'Not my will, but thine be done.' Jesus did that! As he thought about Calvary and the pain of crucifixion and covenant implications of his substitutionary death as the servant of God, he trembled! He wrestled with it and that is profound! He asked if there was some other way! Isn't that astonishing? That he could do that without ever lapsing into the sin of unbelief or unwillingness is too great to comprehend. But he came to rest in contentment in God's unfolding providence for him: your will be done! And as soon as he had said that, he said to his disciples in the Garden of Gethsemane, 'Rise, let us go from here' (John 14:31).

That is what this psalm is saying. Don't quarrel with God's will, don't fight it, don't resist it, but yield to it. See that in everything that you do, every day that you live, God is around you, guarding, upholding and defending you.

God defends and protects. Did you notice that lovely picture in verse 2? It is just here that he uses a beautiful picture of giving sleep to his beloved. Some of you know this; God makes you unafraid of what may loom in the darkness, or of the threat of disease and death. Now it may be that what the psalmist is saying is something slightly different from what it may first appear to be. It is not that he makes us sleep as much as he continues to give, to provide, and watch over us while we sleep.

Isn't that beautiful?

While you sleep, God is awake and sustaining the universe, and the course of your life! Here is a picture of a man who is so distressed that he is eating the bread of sorrows! He's feeding on depression! He's gloomy and looking on the dark side of everything. And the psalmist says, 'Stop! Stop! He gives his beloved sleep!' Or perhaps, he gives (provides) while they sleep.

Do you know that verse in Deuteronomy 32:11? It's about the eagle, and the way it sometimes forces the young ones to fly, pushing them out of the nest, and allowing them to fall towards the ground. Then swooping down, the eagle catches them before they hit the ground!

God moves in a mysterious way...

Adoniram Judson once wrote, 'The future is as bright as the promises of God.' He was right.

There is one more point for us to see in this psalm: it is that *God loves us*. The proof for this is found in the wonderful little expression at the end of verse 2, 'beloved'. We are loved by God! Do you really think about that? What you are saying whenever you are anxious and troubled is that you do not believe that God loves you or that you are one of his loved ones! You are saying something very different; you are saying that he cannot be trusted, that he is unpredictable, irascible and volatile.

'He who did not spare his own Son but gave him up for us all, how will he not also with him graciously give us all things?' (Rom. 8:32).

For your journal...

1. Are there any circumstances in your life that might lead you to conclude that God has forsaken you? What are they? Why do you think that these circumstances prove this to be so?

2. What are the main features of God's covenants with us? What implications can you draw from the nature of these divine covenants?

3. 'God is in control!' What does this imply for your life?

Psalm 128

A Song of Ascents

1 *Blessed is everyone who fears the LORD,*
    who walks in his ways!
2 *You shall eat the fruit of the labour of your hands;*
    you shall be blessed, and it shall be well with you.

3 *Your wife will be like a fruitful vine*
    within your house;
your children will be like olive shoots
    round your table.
4 *Behold, thus shall the man be blessed*
    who fears the LORD.

5 *The LORD bless you from Zion!*
May you see the prosperity of Jerusalem
    all the days of your life!
6 *May you see your children's children!*
    Peace be upon Israel!

Day 9

Bless this house

> ➤ *Begin by reading Psalm 128.*
> ➤ *Pray about what you have read.*
> ➤ *Make notes on what you think God is teaching you.*
> ➤ *Read the chapter.*
> ➤ *Answer the questions in the section 'For your journal'.*

Psalm 128

> *Bless this house, O Lord, we pray,*
> *Make it safe by night and day.*
> *Bless these walls so firm and stout,*
> *Keeping want and trouble out.*
> *Bless the roof and chimney tall;*
> *Let thy peace lie overall.*
> *Bless this door that it may prove*
> *Ever open to joy and love.*

This piece of doggerel gives wonderful expression to the sentiment contained in this psalm. Like the very first psalm, this one begins with the word 'blessed' (note the many references to 'blessed' and 'bless' in the psalm). It speaks of blessing firstly from the personal and present perspective (vv. 2-4), and then to that of the public and future (vv. 5-6).

In some ways, there is a progression from Psalms 126 – 128 in that Psalm 126 cries out for blessing, 127 tells us that it comes by trusting the Lord, and 128 has a broader scheme of things as its reference: true blessings are covenant blessings in that they come 'from Zion' and 'Jerusalem' (v. 5). It is telling us that it is only those blessings that flow from the house of God that are real and substantial blessings.

This psalm has a timely message for our generation. Ours is a hedonistic age where 'things', the material things which we strive for and seek to gain, are thought to be all-important. The real source of joy and contentment is to be found in the kingdom of God, this psalm tells us. The source of all true hedonism is in fellowship with God. This is what true blessing is. These blessings are experienced in the creation ordinances of work, marriage and worship.

If we look at this psalm a little closer, we will see that the first section concentrates on the personal and the present (vv. 1-4). Its focus is on the sphere of work and of marriage. You will notice something else that often occurs in biblical writings, and especially in the Psalms: verses 1 and 4 are almost identical and form what technicians call an *inclusio*. This acts in a similar fashion to the way bookends do: they encapsulate verses 2 and 3. These bookends tell us something foundational about the entire Christian life: it consists — begins and continues — in *the fear of God*.

As we know from the Proverbs, the fear of the Lord is the beginning of wisdom, the soul of godliness (Prov. 1:7; 9:10; compare Job 28:28; Ps. 111:10). The fear of God is the essence of true piety. Godly people fear God. Over 150 times, the Bible tells us so. When it describes the essence of Job's godliness as he withstands massive onslaughts of pain, loss and suffering, it says that he was a man who feared God (Job 1:1; 2:3). Strange, then, that it is the one characteristic that is so very often missing from contemporary Christianity.

The fear of God consists in a right appreciation of, and response to, who God is. It is the response of a believer to the nature and character of God as he has revealed himself. Principally, it is a response to that quality in God which we identify as his 'god-ness' — that is to say, his greatness and his majesty. It is the sense of awe and wonder that comes when we realize that the God of heaven calls us into fellowship with himself.

The psalms are aware of this a great deal. They extol God's greatness and respond appropriately. 'How great are your works, O LORD!... but you, O LORD, are on high for ever' (Ps. 92:5, 8). 'O LORD my God, you are very great! You are clothed with splendour and majesty,' (Ps. 104:1).

God is not only great, but incomprehensible! It is not that he cannot be known at all, but that he cannot be known *fully*. What we know of him is only a little. To cite a medieval saying: *finitum non capax infiniti* (the finite cannot comprehend the infinite). To grapple with this truth is to reach the point where we appreciate that all true hedonism comes by way of our response to the revelation of Almighty God. So pervasive is this that Peter tells us to live our lives here as 'strangers ... in reverent fear' (1 Peter 1:17, NIV). 'The fear of God is the beginning of wisdom and they that lack the beginning have neither middle nor end,' said John Bunyan.

Why does Psalm 128 begin and end with the fear of God? The parallel in the opening verse explains: the fear of God will keep us 'walking in his ways'. 'The way for us to conform *our* lifestyle to *his* lifestyle', says the psalmist, 'is to fear the Lord.'

We need to think of it in this way: at home and at work all kinds of issues arise that perplex and grieve us. And this is where Job can help us! What did it mean for Job to fear God when all kinds of things were happening in his family and in his business? The answer seems to lie in his *faith*. He trusted God absolutely. He committed everything to him. 'Naked I came from my mother's womb, and naked shall I return. The LORD gave, and the LORD has taken away; blessed be the name of the LORD' (Job 1:21).

That is precisely what Jesus means when he says in John 14:15: 'If you love me, you will keep my commandments.' It is precisely the same categories of thought: fear, love, walking in God's way, keeping God's commandments... If you really fear God then you are committed to walk in his ways no matter what; however dark it gets. Even if the lights go out entirely.

> Thy way not mine, O Lord,
> However dark it be!
> Lead me by thine own hand,
> Choose out the path for me.

Horatius Bonar
1808-1889

This is worked out in three particular areas.

Off to work...

Take a look at verse 2, 'You shall eat the fruit of the labour of your hands; you shall be blessed, and it shall be well with you.' It sounds like a health and wealth gospel, doesn't it? It is easy to see how some people could take it that way. If you walk in God's ways, if you consecrate yourself to him, you will prosper. It all depends on how you understand this word 'prosper'!

The believer who is walking in God's ways will find that work is *in itself* a blessing! Work *is* the prosperity. You will find enjoyment in what God has given you to do. 'Delight yourself in the LORD, and he will give you the desires of your heart' (Ps. 37:4). Whenever success comes, and sometimes it comes in surprising and unexpected ways, it is something *God has given*. He has blessed our efforts. When we see vocation in this wider sense, it is liberating: whatever we do, we do it as unto the Lord, and for his glory. In one sense, at least, *nothing* is secular. The whole of life is lived *coram Deo* — before the face of God!

> O happy home where each one serves Thee, lowly,
> Whatever his appointed work may be,
> Till every common task seems great and holy,
> When it is done, O Lord, as unto Thee!
>
> Carl Johann Philip Spitta's hymn:
> 'O happy home where Thou art loved the dearest'

Do you remember how Paul rebukes those Thessalonians who had begun to think that because the Lord's advent was 'soon' they had no need to work? What does Paul say? 'If anyone is not willing to work, let him not eat' (2 Thess. 3:10). You dare not enjoy the fruit of labour, if you are not willing to engage in work yourself!

Isn't it a blessing to enjoy the fruits of one's labour? It is a wonderful thing when our calling coincides with our inclination. We are to see the provision of *daily bread* as 'prosperity', because we see it as God's reward for labour. Believers who work with integrity and uprightness may pay for it by not getting the contracts that others get because they refuse to offer bribes; and God blesses that. Isn't that prosperity? Isn't that a magnificent example of how God takes care of his own? Being a Christian is no guarantee of wealth! That is a travesty of exegesis! It denies the experience of men like Job, Joseph and Paul, and, for that matter, of *Jesus*!

God provides! He rewards the labour of our hands, time and time again. More than we could ever have imagined!

That's why the New American Standard translation of this verse is so much better, I think. *'It will be well with you.'* It takes into consideration the idea that things are well *with me*, even when all hell is breaking loose around me.

Home, sweet home

The happiness of those who fear the Lord is not only experienced in work, it is experienced in marriage.

It is a sad reality of life in this world that homes are increasingly becoming places of strife and turmoil rather than peace and tranquillity. For many, entering the home is entering a scene of battle and strife. Many can relate the scars which such backgrounds bring.

Have you ever envied the testimony of those raised in 'Christian homes' where parental life seemed altogether idyllic, with stories of praying parents and loving situations? We need to realize, however, that God has brought us to himself in different ways. In his good providence he has moulded and shaped our lives according to an all-wise and sovereign plan that implies a uniqueness about each one of us. There is a reason why he has put us in the families we are a part of.

What we have in this psalm is a picture of the family. It is 'Home, sweet home'. This picture is idealized, as is the picture of work given in verse 2. Here is a husband and wife, and children. Everything about it is ideal and picturesque. God loves family life. He sent his own Son into a loving family home.

Some will find these words difficult. They long that this might be a picture of their lives, but it isn't. Who are they? They are those who are not married, and those who *are* married, but have no children — *cannot have children*! They torture themselves with questions such as: Is there something wrong with me? Have I committed some sin? Is this a divine punishment of some kind?

Jesus was a bachelor, and we must never forget that. Paul was too! The word for some is: *be patient*; and for others: *learn to bow to his sovereign providence*. He never asks anyone to carry a burden that he or she *cannot* carry. He has chosen you to fill up the sufferings of Christ. When God asks for a task to be fulfilled, he provides the means to accomplish it.

The point of this psalm is the blessing of a fruitful wife. Some husbands need to pause and reflect on it for a moment. Have *you* lost sight of the blessing that *your wife* is? When did you last really thank God for her? Wives can do the same for their husbands, of course, even though the psalm is reflecting on motherhood. The Bible places a great honour upon childbearing: 'she will be saved through childbearing — if they continue in faith and love and holiness, with self-control' (1 Tim. 2:15).

Can you remember the blessing you felt when those first children began to appear, and you were living in an apartment unsure where to put everything? Things may be very different now. You may be dwelling in grander accommodation, for a start! But, do you think that the psalmist is really so insensitive as to suggest that what he really thinks you should be living in is a *mansion*? Some of us can look back and recount with special

affection the sheer blessing and happiness we enjoyed in the
first home we lived in when newly married with children on
the way. And there was only enough money to see us through
a week or two!

Worship the King

In verses 4 and 5, the psalmist has moved from the present to
the future. These verses recognize that, ultimately, all blessings
come 'from Zion', or 'from Jerusalem'. What does this mean?
These are names associated with the place where God was
worshipped. Remember, these are Psalms of Ascent where
more than likely the psalmist was in Jerusalem, attending one
of the great worship services of the Old Testament calendar.
As he did so, he would come to the realization that all blessing
comes from one's relationship to God's people and to the
place where he is worshipped. As the people of God assemble
for worship, his blessings are communicated.

'It is good to give thanks to the LORD, to sing praises to your
name, O Most High' (Ps. 92:1). Man's chief end is to glorify
God and to enjoy him for ever. Sinners who are restored to
fellowship with God are conscious of a sense of satisfaction
unequalled by anything this world affords. 'So I will bless you
as long as I live; in your name I will lift up my hands. My soul
will be satisfied as with fat and rich food, and my mouth will
praise you with joyful lips' (Ps. 63:4-5).

Joy springs from knowing that we are no longer what we
were — we are a new creation (2 Cor. 5:17). Sin has been
forgiven, justification acquired, and adoption bestowed.
Joy emanates from what every Christian feels whenever he
worships God: somehow he is sharing in the powers of the
world to come (Heb. 6:5). Sometimes, we are conscious of

being in another world: in the very presence of God. In that sense the psalmist is echoing the words of a hymn by John Newton, 'Glorious things of thee are spoken, Zion city of our God...' when it says, 'solid joys and lasting treasures, none but Zion's children know'. All other experiences of joy and happiness are ephemeral and transitory by comparison.

> Saviour, if of Zion's city
> I, through grace a member am,
> Let the world deride or pity,
> I will glory in Thy name.
> Fading is the worldling's pleasure,
> All his boasted pomp and show;
> Solid joys and lasting treasure
> None but Zion's children know.[1]

John Newton
1725-1807

Thomas Brooks, puritan author of *Precious Remedies Against Satan's Devices*, impresses upon us the importance of doing what God tells us in the Bible. If you don't put into practice what you know, then why listen to the Word of God? If his words to you, today, are about forgiveness and his help for the repentant sinner, then these words will lash you if you don't obey them.

When asked what the first requirement of an orator was, the Greek orator Demosthenes answered, '*Action.*' When asked what the second part was, he answered, '*Action.*' And the third part, his answer was still, '*Action.*'

So it is with listening to sermons. What is the most important part?

It is doing what we have been told to do!

What is the next important part?

It is also doing what we have been told to do.

And what is the next most important part?

It is still doing what we have been told to do.

For your journal...

1. Take some moments to reflect on your home. What are the things for which you are thankful? What are the things that concern you the most?

2. What have you learned about fearing God? Make a list of those areas in your life that are affected by your response to this.

3. Are you applying biblical principles to the way you do your daily work? Are there ways in which you could improve your witness here?

4. If you have children, spend extra time praying for them today. Make a covenant with God to pray for them at the turn of every hour today. (If you do not have children of your own, then pray for your siblings.)

Psalm 129

A Song of Ascents

1 *'Greatly have they afflicted me from my youth' —*
let Israel now say —
2 *'Greatly have they afflicted me from my youth,*
yet they have not prevailed against me.
3 *The ploughers ploughed upon my back;*
they made long their furrows.'
4 *The LORD is righteous;*
he has cut the cords of the wicked.
5 *May all who hate Zion*
be put to shame and turned backwards!
6 *Let them be like the grass on the housetops,*
which withers before it grows up,
7 *with which the reaper does not fill his hand*
nor the binder of sheaves his arms,
8 *nor do those who pass by say,*
'The blessing of the LORD be upon you!
We bless you in the name of the LORD!'

Day 10

The Lord is righteous

> ➤ *Begin by reading Psalm 129.*
> ➤ *Pray about what you have read.*
> ➤ *Make notes on what you think God is teaching you.*
> ➤ *Read the chapter.*
> ➤ *Answer the questions in the section 'For your journal'.*

Psalm 129

What are we to make of the closing verses of this psalm? The psalmist seems to be praying an *imprecation* — that is, that a *curse* fall upon those who have been persecuting him. Are such prayers as these really 'devilish' as, for example, C. S. Lewis wrote?[1] Other commentators are adamant that such prayers as these are 'not the oracles of God', and are 'quite unsuitable for the church'. What are we to make of them?

What is said here, of course, is fairly mild in comparison to some other psalms (109 and 137, for example), but all the same, the psalmist doesn't want anyone to pronounce a blessing on these people. What are we to make of it? How can a psalm like this be material for our devotions? Isn't this something we should hurriedly pass over, excusing the psalmist for his outbursts and saying, 'Well, we are all human after all'? This is hardly how we should respond!

Of course, Bible commentators have spilled ink over these things. Some have suggested that these verses are not the inspired Word of God, but the vengeance and spite of a man who has been hurt. We can understand such sentiments, of course, but we are in no way to endorse them. Jesus tells us to turn the other cheek and to forgive seventy times seven (Matt. 5:39; 18:22).

Others point out that God 'allows' all kinds of immoral practices (for example, polygamy) to go unchecked in the Old Testament. These imprecations are just another example of the primitive quality of Old Testament ethics. The more mature expression of what God intends is to be found in the pages of the New Testament. But, will this stand scrutiny? What about the book of Revelation? There are similar cries for vengeance there, too. 'O Sovereign Lord … how long…?' the martyrs cry (Rev. 6:10). They want God to come and judge their executioners. Such 'prayers' will mean that Revelation will also need to be removed from the 'acceptable' canon.

What are we to make of these prayers? Are we to dismiss these verses as an expression of personal vengeance, in which the psalmist 'just looses his cool' and blurts out something he should not. If so, our task is to try to discern what is truly inspired and what is not. It is not as simple as that, of course; evangelical interpreters don't deny inspiration here any more than when the Scripture cites the words of Satan in Genesis 3. The issue is not inspiration, but interpretation; does God approve of what is written here, even if the Holy Spirit did faithfully record every detail of the psalmist's personal vengeance? The problem, if there is one, is that the New Testament itself cites these very psalms without any hint of embarrassment! Peter, for example, cites the imprecatory Psalm 109, and applies it to Judas when they are appointing his successor (Acts 1:20). Can we say with Spurgeon, 'If this be an imprecation, let it stand; for our heart says "Amen" to it'?

The answer to this 'problem' is best found by dealing with the entire psalm in its own context. Looking at the psalm overall, we see it immediately falls into two sections. In verses 1-4, the verbs are all in the past tense. In verses 5-8, the verbs are all in the future. Obviously, the psalmist is looking backward and then looking forward. He is looking forward and uttering something based upon what has occurred in the past.

The God who blesses

The first thing to notice about this psalm is the way in which the opening verses seem to suggest some kind of liturgical setting.

'Greatly have they afflicted me from my youth' —
    let Israel now say —
'Greatly have they afflicted me from my youth,
    yet they have not prevailed against me.'

It is pure conjecture, of course, but was the psalmist encouraging the congregation to join in with him and make this *their* song, as well as his? In any case, this is a psalm, not simply of an individual, but of the entire community of God's people. In that case, what is being said is something of the history of Israel rather than the personal history of the psalmist. The use of the first person is therefore stylistic.

What these words are testifying to is the fact that 'affliction' has been a factor of Israel's existence from the beginning. From the time when Israel had been treated 'ruthlessly' (Exod. 1:13) until now, life had been hard for the people of God. The psalm is giving voice to the basic biblical principle that wherever the kingdom of God manifests itself, there is always opposition. It is the outworking of that principle that we first encounter in Genesis 3; the seed of the serpent is at war with the seed of the woman. That is how we are to understand what is going on in the pages of the Old Testament; and, for that matter, in the Bible as a whole.

The psalm employs a striking metaphor in verse 3: 'The ploughers ploughed upon my back; they made long their furrows.' This may well refer to the experience of whipping that the slaves received in Egypt. Less likely is the suggestion that this psalm describes the period of Israel's exile in Babylon where such treatment was perhaps common, too.

Suffering was a part of the history of the church in the Old Testament as it has been for the church in the New Testament. The cross is the way to life, suffering the way to victory. We are not surprised when we pass through many tribulations. Several New Testament books, such as 1 and 2 Peter and Revelation, are specifically written to warn the church of impending trouble for those who follow in the footsteps of Jesus Christ.

But what deliverance can we expect from trouble? Trouble will come, but is there any word of assurance and hope? Listen to the psalmist: 'Greatly have they afflicted me from my youth, yet they have not prevailed against me.' And again in verse 4, he says, 'The LORD is righteous; he has cut the cords of the wicked.'

However great the trouble (verses 1 and 2: 'greatly'), there had been great deliverances. That is the lesson of Israel's history. But, of course, it is more than that. There had been deliverances from Egypt, from the Philistines, from Assyria, from Babylon, and later from Rome; but the focus does not fall on the deliverance. The focus falls on the *one* who delivers: 'The LORD is righteous' (v. 4).

All our problems stem from a failure to focus on God. That is true as far as our personal lives are concerned, as well as the corporate life of the church. Again and again, the Bible turns us back to this simple fact: our chief end is to glorify God.

> 'Oh, children,' said the Lion, 'I feel my strength coming back to me. Oh, children, catch me if you can!' He stood for a second, his eyes very bright, his limbs quivering, lashing himself with his tail. Then he made a leap high over their heads and landed on the other side of the Table. Laughing, though she didn't know why, Lucy scrambled over to reach him. Aslan leaped again. A mad chase began. Round and round the hill-top he led them, now hopelessly out of their reach, now letting them almost catch his tail, now diving between them, now tossing them in the air with his huge and beautifully velveted paws and catching them again, and now stopping unexpectedly so that all three of them rolled over together in a happy heap of fur and arms and legs. It was such a romp as no one has ever had except in Narnia; and whether it was more like playing with a thunderstorm or playing with a kitten Lucy never could make up her mind.
>
> C. S. Lewis, *The Lion, the Witch and the Wardrobe*[2]

What does the word 'righteous' mean when applied to God? You will remember the debate that Luther had, for example, at the time of the Reformation over the expression 'the righteousness of God' in the first chapter of Romans and how

he came to say at one point, that he 'hated' the righteousness of
God. Luther had perceived God's righteousness as something
which God demanded of him and which he (Luther) couldn't
supply. The answer to his dilemma was an understanding of
the great biblical doctrines of substitution and imputation.
God imputes to the account of the one who exercises faith in
Jesus Christ the righteousness he requires!

What does the righteousness of God mean in Psalm 129?

In Psalm 129, God's righteousness fills the psalmist with
confidence of deliverance from his enemies. How does it do
that? Would not the thought that God is righteous add to his
sense of unease and discomfort? Not only is he surrounded
by enemies, but God also threatens to undo him by his
righteousness. How can the psalmist draw comfort from this
assertion of God's character?

The answer is to understand that it is not his own
righteousness that the psalmist is speaking about, but God's.
'God is righteous' implies that he conforms to a standard, *his
own standard*! He is trustworthy and dependable. He keeps
his covenant with his people. Having revealed himself as the
Saviour of his people and the conqueror of his foes, he never
deviates from that standard. No matter what happens, God is
never going to abrogate his promise. *That* is something we can
utterly depend upon.

God had made the promise of a Messiah to Israel. That is
why he cared for her and protected her. That is why he chas-
tised her whenever she rebelled against him. And God is going
to keep that promise. That was why Daniel could pray as he
did in Daniel 9. He had just read a promise in Jeremiah in his
personal devotions! 'Lord, do as you have said that you would
do' — that's what that great prayer in Daniel 9 is all about!

The first part of this psalm is saying to us that our sense of
gratitude is often diminished by our failure to respond to the

character of God. The Lord delivers his people because he is righteous!

Think of it! As God's children, we have been set free from bondage to sin by the emancipating power of the gospel of Jesus Christ! God has broken the cords which shackled us. In Charles Wesley's words:

Long my imprisoned spirit lay
Fast bound in sin and nature's night;
Thine eye diffused a quickening ray,
I woke, the dungeon flamed with light;
My chains fell off, my heart was free,
I rose, went forth, and followed Thee.

Can you sing this song in your hearts? It is a 'new song' of deliverance and victory in battle (see Ps. 40:3). Can you sing an even greater song — one which you find echoes of in the book of Revelation? It is the song of the redeemed who have triumphed, because God is righteous. He will have victory over every foe: the beast of the sea and the beast of the land, the antichrist and the false prophet. 'Fallen, fallen is Babylon the great!' (Rev. 18:2).

'Worthy are you, our Lord and God,
    to receive glory and honour and power,
for you created all things,
    and by your will they existed and were created'
                                                    (Rev. 4:11).

'Worthy is the Lamb who was slain,
    to receive power and wealth and wisdom and might
    and honour and glory and blessing!'
                                                    (Rev. 5:12).

'Amen!
Blessing and glory
and wisdom and thanksgiving and honour
and power and might
be to our God for ever and ever!
Amen'

(Rev. 7:12).

The God who curses

We have noted that the expression 'the LORD is righteous'
assures deliverance for his people. God remembers his
covenant promises and rescues his people from bondage and
tyranny. He brings about the promised salvation of which the
Bible speaks from Genesis 3 onwards.

But this implies a two-edged understanding of righteousness. God's covenant has blessings *and* curses. If salvation is to
be won, an enemy has to be defeated. If sin is to be forgiven,
justice has to be satisfied. If a Saviour is sent into the world,
Satan is defeated. The covenant is *always* double-edged. That
is what is so moving about Christ's prayer in Gethsemane. If
Jesus were going to save us, if God's will and promise were
going to be fulfilled, he would have to become the *cursed
one*. The covenant curse would come down upon him and he
would be severed from fellowship with his Father. That is why
Jesus trembled. He did not fear death so much as he feared
God's wrath! He feared the *retributive* righteousness of God.
Gethsemane makes no sense apart from this understanding of
it.

It is in this light that we are to make sense of these imprecations in verses 5-8. We are not to think of them as expressions
of personal revenge. No! The Bible is very clear about the

impropriety of personal vengeance. It is always wrong! It is a sin. It is a violation of the biblical ethic of being a good neighbour. We are to turn the other cheek. We are go the second and third mile. We are to forgive, seventy times seven. That is the biblical ethic for individual conduct. If someone does me wrong, I am never right to take things into my own hands and seek to do ill to that person. On the contrary, we are to love that person even if that costs us more pain. The Bible is very clear about that.

So what is going on here? There are two things in particular:

a. This is a corporate expression and not an individual one. The psalmist is adopting a much broader perspective. He has the life and testimony of the entire community in view here.

b. He is expressing his zeal, not because *he* has been offended or hurt; God's name has been impugned. *His* honour is on the line. He is grieved and troubled because people are not honouring God as they should be. That is his supreme concern. Our problem is that we are often so concerned about ourselves and our reputation that we miss the big picture: the honour of God. There is nothing more important than that — nothing!

What the psalmist writes is that those who refuse to honour God should be punished. Ultimately, the curse of God should come down upon them. That is what the psalmist is saying in these verses. Is it wrong to say that, to pray that?

Consider what it is we are doing when we pray the Lord's Prayer. We recite it, perhaps, unthinkingly. Some have rejected its frequent use in public worship because of this very danger. Think of that petition: 'Your kingdom come...' (Matt. 6:10;

Luke 11:2). What exactly are we asking for? Think about it! We are asking that the kingdom of God come in all its fulness, that the purposes of God be fulfilled. That is not just a prayer for the growth of the church and for people to be saved. It is a prayer that Christ would come again, that the Judgement Day be inaugurated; that the sheep be separated from the goats; that the saved find eternal rest in heaven; and that the unconverted be cast into hell. That is what we are praying for. That *is* God's purpose, and we must never forget it! There is a hell, and it isn't going to be empty. The wicked who have set themselves against God and his purposes will be there. They are under the control of their master Satan. This is why Jesus came into the world, so that he might destroy the works of the devil (1 John 3:8). Perhaps we don't think of it that way, but that is what we are praying for when we desire the consummation of the purposes of God with respect to his kingdom.

If that is so, why doesn't the New Testament ever express imprecations in the same way that the Old Testament does? Consider some verses from the New Testament: 'If anyone has no love for the Lord, let him be accursed' (1 Cor. 16:22). Isn't that precisely what the psalmist is saying? 'Let not a blessing come upon him.'

Consider what Paul says of Alexander the coppersmith who had done him much harm, 'The Lord will repay him according to his deeds' (2 Tim. 4:14). What does he mean by 'the Lord will repay him...'? Paul goes on to warn Timothy about this man, because he is as much opposed to Timothy's message as he has been to Paul's.

What we have here can be summarized along three lines of thought:

a. Imprecations form a part of our desire for justice whenever a wrong has been committed. God desires justice, and there is nothing at all at odds with desiring justice. Whenever a great wrong has been committed against a person, it isn't necessarily the Christian response simply to say, 'I forgive you!' That can leave the person who has committed the offence without a clear impression of the wrong that has been done. Forgiveness and repentance go together, like a hand and a glove. We want reconciliation, but not at any cost. There has to be an acknowledgement of wrongdoing. Justice and love always go together. God forgives our sin, but not without punishing it in his own Son instead.

b. Vengeance belongs to God. That is the clear testimony of Scripture. These are prayers for God to act, not for the psalmist or some vigilante to take things into their own hands. A Christian who is taken up with personal spite and spends his or her time plotting and conniving revenge is a sorry sight. 'Vengeance is mine, I will repay, says the Lord' (Rom. 12:19).

c. There ought to be a desire for the name of God to be glorified in the salvation of his people as well as the judgement of his enemies. We are involved in a war! As Christians, we declare all-out war against Satan and his kingdom. God's kingdom cannot come without the destruction of the kingdom of Satan. If sinners stand in the way of God's purpose to save, they will be destroyed.

'Study a chapter from *Foxe's Book of Martyrs*,' wrote Spurgeon, 'and see if you do not feel inclined to read an imprecatory psalm over Bishop Bonner or Bloody Mary. It may be that some wretched nineteenth-century sentimentalist will blame you; if so, then read another one over him!'[3]

Can you pray such prayers when you realize all this?

It is a mark of maturity.

For your journal...

1. Explain in as much detail as you can what it means to say, 'The LORD is righteous.'

2. Think of how you might respond to the imprecation of this psalm. Can you pray something like this? Write it down, look at it and ask yourself, 'Is this something God would have me say in prayer?'

Psalm 130

A Song of Ascents

1 *Out of the depths I cry to you, O LORD!*
2   *O Lord, hear my voice!*
Let your ears be attentive
      to the voice of my pleas for mercy!

3 *If you, O LORD, should mark iniquities,*
      O Lord, who could stand?
4 *But with you there is forgiveness,*
      that you may be feared.

5 *I wait for the LORD, my soul waits,*
      and in his word I hope;
6 *my soul waits for the Lord*
      more than watchmen for the morning,
      more than watchmen for the morning.

7 *O Israel, hope in the LORD!*
      For with the LORD there is steadfast love,
      and with him is plentiful redemption.
8 *And he will redeem Israel*
      from all his iniquities.

Day 11

Out of the depths

> ➤ *Begin by reading Psalm 130.*
> ➤ *Pray about what you have read.*
> ➤ *Make notes on what you think God is teaching you.*
> ➤ *Read the chapter.*
> ➤ *Answer the questions in the section 'For your journal'.*

Psalm 130

On one occasion, at Coburg (during the *Diet of Augsburg* where the relationship of the emerging Protestant church to the church of Rome was becoming clearer), Luther told his friends, 'Come, let us sing that psalm, "Out of the depths..." in derision of the devil!'

There is a connection between this psalm and the previous one: it is the righteousness of God (129:4). If God sides with his people, then all is well and nothing can ultimately dislodge them from their communion with him. Whatever their enemies may scheme, their plots amount to nothing: '... they have not prevailed against me' (129:2).

But, there is another concern. If God stands amongst his people in all his resplendent righteousness, will that not expose their sin and cause them even more trouble than their enemies are capable of doing? Will they not be condemned in God's presence?

De profundis.

That's what this psalm is often called, after the Latin for 'Out of the depths'. Luther was once asked at table which psalms he thought might be the best. His answer? The 'Pauline psalms' was his reply. When pressed to identify them, he answered, 'Psalms 32, 51, 130 and 143'.

You can immediately see why he should have identified Psalm 130 as 'Pauline'. It is about a man who is convicted of his sin before the righteousness of God and discovers that 'there is forgiveness'. That is the greatest discovery of all.

There are four sections to the psalm, each one marked by a key word (or words):

In the depths!

The first section marks the *condition* of the psalmist. It is signalled by the expression 'in the depths', and the word that comes at the end of verse 2: 'mercy'.

Here is a man in trouble. He is in the depths! And the reason for his despair is given to us in verses 3 and 8; it is because of his sins. We may not fully appreciate this, especially if we are in the habit of making light of our sins. Taking sin seriously is a perspective with which Bible readers become accustomed. A book written by one of the Puritans, Ralph Venning, who was ejected from his living in 1662, once bore the title, *The Plague of Plagues*. It is now called *The Sinfulness of Sin*! That says it all, doesn't it? There is a *sinfulness* about sin that we need to appreciate.

When J. C. Ryle came to write his best-selling volume, *Holiness*, he began with a chapter on 'sin'. The opening words are, 'He that wishes to attain right views about Christian holiness, must begin by examining the vast and solemn subject of sin.'[1] That is where this psalm begins.

'Sin', says the *Shorter Catechism*, 'is any want of conformity unto, or transgression of, the law of God.' It is the smallest infringement of the law! It is the least deficiency in reflecting the image of God!

This psalmist is someone who appreciates the fact that before the righteousness of God, he is unrighteous. These two, God and man, cannot live side by side, not unless something is done about sin. Sin deserves punishment. And that is what this psalmist is saying: he is guilty before God and he knows it.

Three things follow.

Firstly, God alone has the remedy to this problem of sin. In one sense, the Lord *is* the problem! Do you see that? It is the very righteousness and integrity of the Lord that causes the problem. If God were to wink at sin; if God were simply to ignore it, or deal with it less severely; if he didn't threaten a Day of Judgement, then, there would not be a *problem* of sin.

Sin is *a problem that needs to be dealt with*! Have you come to that point in your relationship with God? And if so, have you seen, as this psalm so beautifully demonstrates, that this is a problem that you take to God! Yes, God *is* the problem and God *is* also the solution! What the psalmist needs is *mercy*. And this is something that can only come from God. He is the one who is offended by our sin, and he is the one who confers mercy. We must bring our sins *to the Lord*!

Secondly, God hears the faintest cry. Note what the psalmist says in verse 2, 'Hear my voice…' Doesn't that suggest to you that God is listening to the very *sound* of his prayer? What kind of prayer (*sound*) does a man who is in the depths cry? When you are in despair, when you are feeling so low that you wonder if you will ever be rescued, what kind of cry do you think emerges? It may be just a sigh or a groan! But God hears the faintest cry of the most despairing soul! There is no whisper that God cannot hear.

Thirdly, there are no extremities too deep for the Lord. There is another psalm which speaks of 'deep calls to deep' (Ps. 42:7). It depicts a man in almost total despair. And yet, no matter how low he may feel, how sinful he may be, how great his sins are, the psalmist still feels he can come before the Lord and ask for mercy. It is the same here.

Do you remember those Apollo space missions to the moon? There would be times when the radio signal would be lost because the spacecraft was on the 'dark side' of the moon. For several minutes, there would be no communication. In our own time, there are occasions when cell (or mobile) phones cannot pick up a signal. That is never the case with the Lord. Whatever our condition, we may be assured that God knows about it. We can bring it to him. We can pray ourselves out of it. We can take our sins, however ugly they may be, to the Lord and plead for mercy!

The assurance of forgiveness

The psalmist is preaching to himself! He finds himself in this condition, conscious of God's righteousness and his own sinfulness, and he tells himself something about God. He thinks about the possibility of God keeping a record of his sins. 'If you, O LORD, should mark iniquities...' (v. 3).

God does keep a record — of everything! There are ledgers and databases containing the records of all our sins: our public and private sins, our habitual sins and our 'secret' sins (secret, that is, to others, but not to God). God knows everything that we do and there is coming a day when all of this will be revealed. What the psalmist is thinking about here is not that God knows them and records them, but that God will keep a record *against* us. In that case, there is nothing we can do. We are doomed. There is nowhere to hide from the all-searching gaze of his holiness.

> O child of God, this grief
> That bows your spirit low
> Is yours but half, for Christ Himself
> Still shares His people's woe.
>
> His wisdom planned it out
> Then bore it on His heart
> Till gently on your untried back
> Love laid the lesser part.
>
> So take it all with joy,
> Together bear the cross,
> For while you suffer He distils
> A heaven from your loss.
>
> Beneath His secret will
> Subscribe with ready pen,
> Add to this sorrow God has sent
> A resolute 'Amen'.
>
> Each day spend out in faith,
> Nor prove His labour vain;
> Cast still on Christ the pressing weight
> Who only can sustain.
>
> Faith Cook, *Grace in Winter: Rutherford in Verse*[2]

Here is the amazing thing: God forgives penitent sinners! '...with you there is forgiveness' (Ps. 130:4).

John Owen, the Congregationalist puritan of the seventeenth century, at a very difficult time in his life, wrote a treatise (a commentary) on this psalm, and in particular on this verse, 'But with you there is forgiveness, that you may be feared' (v. 4). It is one of the finest expositions of this psalm available. At a time when Owen was doubting his salvation and lacking assurance, when the devil was suggesting to him that his sins were so great that God couldn't possibly forgive them, the words of this psalm proved of immense help to him.

God forgives all kinds of sins, all quantities of sins. Let's think about that for a moment. What about adultery? It is a vile sin. It is a betrayal of trust and of one's word. There is no excuse for it. It is a sin against a spouse and a sin against God. Yet, for the penitent sinner, like David, there is forgiveness. Listen to him in Psalm 32, and note the sense of joy he has in God's forgiveness.

> Blessed is the one whose transgression is forgiven,
>   whose sin is covered.
> Blessed is the man against whom the LORD counts no
>   iniquity,
>   and in whose spirit there is no deceit
>
> (vv. 1-2).

Remember how Jesus spoke to a woman caught in adultery with these breathtaking words, 'Neither do I condemn you; go, and from now on sin no more' (John 8:11).

What are we to say about murder? Do you recall the beautiful words to the dying thief, 'Today you will be with me in paradise' (Luke 23:43)? Is there anything more sublime in all of the Scriptures?

I have said that this is a Pauline psalm. Do you remember how Paul could say at one point that he was the 'foremost' of sinners (1 Tim. 1:15)? Can a blasphemer of Jesus Christ be forgiven? Yes, he can! Can a persecutor of the church, who has been a vile and offensive person, be forgiven? Yes, he can! There is forgiveness with God!

Waiting patiently

'I wait for the LORD, my soul waits … my soul waits' (vv. 5-6).

Interpreters vary as to what these verses mean. Because they think that forgiveness is certain and already acquired at this point in the psalm, some want to see this as the psalmist waiting in confidence. He is basking in the graciousness of God. There's something about that that's appealing, isn't there? We ought to bask in the goodness of God to us. We ought to wait upon him, patiently acknowledging his kindness and mercy to us in the gospel. We ought to do far more of that.

Others think that the psalmist is saying something a little different. He is assured that God forgives; but, forgiveness hasn't yet been received. He has to 'wait' for it. In a sense, we always have to wait for it, because forgiveness isn't to be taken for granted. That's the problem in the church today, isn't it? Forgiveness is cheap. It is so easy to get, that when it comes it doesn't mean very much. We can go on sinning just as we have done, in the certainty that we can always return and get some more forgiveness later.

The psalmist seems peculiarly conscious of the price of forgiveness. He uses the language of 'redemption' (v. 7). There are two words in Hebrew which are translated redemption, or redeem, and this one focuses on the *cost* of redemption. Its cost is the death of Jesus, the Son of God.

There was no other good enough
    to pay the price of sin;
He only could unlock the gate
    of heaven, and let us in.

(Cecil Alexander
'There is a green hill far away', 1847)

Don't you think the psalmist is saying that? Forgiveness is
at the heart of God's covenant dealings with us. Before we can
receive it, we must wait on the sovereign Lord to bestow it.
Forgiveness is something God grants.

Do you note how he puts it? 'I wait for the LORD, my soul
waits … my soul waits…' (vv. 5-6). And in verse 5 he uses
the word 'hope' in a similar way. Do you remember those
wonderful verses in the Bible that speak about 'waiting'?

Wait for the LORD;
    be strong, and let your heart take courage;
    wait for the LORD!

(Ps. 27:14).

'Waiting' in the Bible means exactly what it says here in
Psalm 130:5. It means having confidence in the promises of
God's Word. Look at the word he uses in verse 7, translated
'unfailing love' (NIV). It is an attempt to render a very
precious Hebrew word, *chesed*. It is the word most associated
with God's covenant love. Here is a man who has read God's
promises about salvation and forgiveness and he has assurance!
He's confident! He takes his sins and rests in the promise of
God that he will be forgiven. God forgives because, in his Son,
he has promised to forgive. He forgives *for Jesus' sake*!

But then there is 'watching'. The imagery is very graphic
indeed. It is the figure of a man looking to the horizon for the

first signs of light which will indicate that his shift will be over. He wants to go home to his family and, perhaps, to his bed. He's waiting in eager expectation for that first sign of dawn. The psalmist is waiting with even greater anticipation. He's waiting for the forgiveness of his heavenly Father!

Perhaps there's something even more profound at work here. The imagery of the morning is what theologians call *eschatological*. He's waiting for the fulness, that experience of total forgiveness that can only come in the life hereafter. He's waiting for the Day of the Lord to dawn: the coming of Jesus Christ in glory and triumph at the end of the age, and the beginning of the new heavens and the new earth. He's waiting for that.

He knows he's going to be there.

> Standing on the promises of Christ my King,
> Through eternal ages let his praises ring;
> Glory in the highest, I will shout and sing,
> Standing on the promises of God...

His worship has brought him to that hope.

Corporate redemption

'O Israel...' (v. 7). Think of this as a call, from one who has come to experience the grace of the gospel, on behalf of others that they might experience it, too. There is hope for all who come to God the way the psalmist has come to him. How do we know that? We know that because there are two companions that God always has at his side: *unfailing love* and *full redemption*! There is the love of God and the efficacious sacrifice of Christ.

Everything is ready! Jesus said it in that parable where he bids his servants to go out into the highways and byways, and compel those they meet to come to the supper that is prepared: 'Everything is ready' (Matt. 22:4). God could not be more loving and Christ could not have offered more — the readiness of God and the resources of God!

We have no other argument
We need no other plea
It is enough that Jesus died
And that he died for me.

(Charles Wesley
'Jesus! The Name high over all', 1749)

For your journal…

1. Spend some time thinking about particular sins over which you have made little progress. Why is this? What steps have you made to destroy these sins?

2. 'But with you there is forgiveness; that you may be feared' (v. 4). Think of ways in which this might be applicable to your life.

3. What did you learn about 'waiting' on the Lord today?

Psalm 131

A Song of Ascents. Of David.

1   O LORD, my heart is not lifted up;
         my eyes are not raised too high;
     I do not occupy myself with things
         too great and too marvellous for me.
2   But I have calmed and quietened my soul,
         like a weaned child with its mother;
         like a weaned child is my soul within me.

3   O Israel, hope in the LORD
         from this time forth and for evermore.

Day 12

A weaned soul

➤ *Begin by reading Psalm 131.*
➤ *Pray about what you have read.*
➤ *Make notes on what you think God is teaching you.*
➤ *Read the chapter.*
➤ *Answer the questions in the section 'For your journal'.*

Psalm 131

At first glance, this psalm appears to be a little strange. Like Psalms 133 and 134, Psalm 131 is only three verses long! Whatever the psalm is saying, it says it in brief compass!

But, it is not simply its brevity that stands out; *what* it says is also a little peculiar. Take, for instance, the statement in the opening verse: 'I do not occupy myself with things too great.' Can the psalmist possibly be suggesting that to be overly concerned with theological difficulties is a bad thing? Is the psalm giving expression to the much vaunted spirit of our age, that piety consists in *doing* rather than *knowing*; that the problem with the church today is that it wants too many

Bible studies and not enough practical living? That is hardly the case! Nowhere does the Bible ever pit theology against practice in the way we moderns tend to do.

We shall have to dig a little deeper than that to find out the true meaning of what the psalmist is talking about here. As we do so we shall discover that something of a crisis has taken place in his life. There is a link between this psalm and the previous one; it revolves around the word 'hope' (130:5,7; 131:3). In Psalm 130, confidence arises out of what is true of the Lord, namely, his 'steadfast love' (130:7). In this psalm, confidence arises from something the psalmist experiences in a personal way. He has proven something to be true in his own life; the psalmist now urges others to know it, too.

Do you know that in your life? Has something you have experienced of the character of Almighty God affected you so much that you desire your friends to know it, too?

Psalm 131 is a psalm about Christian maturity. It tells us that the Christian life is one of growth and development, and that the essence of maturity is an experience of being 'calm' and 'quiet'. The psalmist is telling us that he has emerged from one stage of life in which he was dependent, to another in which he describes himself as a 'weaned child'.

In Hebrew society, weaning often took place as late as four or five years of age. The process would involve a certain amount of conscious difficulty in which a child would learn contentment in fending for himself. The process required a change of diet from milk to solid foods; but, it also required a degree of social adjustment in which a child would learn to make certain judgements and choices on his own. It is this process of maturity that provides the focus of attention in this brief, but instructive psalm.

The nature of contentment

The experience of contentment is a spiritual one, but other factors impinge upon it, too. Temperament is one, for example. Some are naturally placid, while others bear a frenetic quality to their personality. We are all different and in some ways this reflects the glory of God's creation. Some are hardly annoyed by anything; others fly into a state of frustration or anger over the most minor mishaps. Personalities vary in much the same way as people's homes do. Some of us live in homes that bear all the marks of a weekend burglary. Others manage to live in homes that would make wonderful articles for a coffee-table book called *Ideal Home and Gardens*.

What is being described here in Psalm 131 is a weaning process, but one that has little to do with temperament. It has to do with faith and maturity. We are meant to imagine something of what that might well involve: tantrums, cries of despair, sudden outbursts of defiance, and so on. Learning to be independent can be a very difficult process, indeed.

God intends to make his children resemble the image of his Son, Jesus Christ. Becoming 'like him' is what the Christian life is all about (1 John 3:2). Interestingly, for Paul, this especially meant becoming 'like him in his death' (Phil. 3:10). Everything that happens in the unfolding providence of God is part of that overall plan to cause us to conform to the pattern of Jesus-like attributes and qualities. Sins have to be mortified; patterns of Adamic rebellion have to be changed; the blueprint of Christ's beauty needs to be stamped upon the soul. All of this can be a difficult and painful process. God uses all kinds of armoury in order to accomplish it. The process of sculpting an image involves painful blows. The pathway to maturity is strewn with obstacles.

It is for this very reason that Paul could say, when writing to the Philippians, that he had 'learned' in whatsoever state he was in to be content (Phil. 4:11). It is interesting that Jesus is said to have 'learned obedience through what he suffered' (Heb. 5:8). He learned to count the cost of obeying his Father in heaven. Interesting, too, is the way we see Jesus put into practice the disciplines of grace (prayer, Bible reading, Scripture memorization, fellowship, to name a few).

Gifted children who show promise in athletics or music must practise certain skills endlessly to ensure that they reach the maturity they aspire to, thereby forming habits and reflexes that will pay dividends when under stress. The routine is arduous, but doing things over and over again is the only way to ensure proficiency.

Holiness is achieved in a similar way. The fact that Paul could say that he 'learned' contentment, gives us the clue as to how painful the *process* of maturity is. Paul was not, I think, a naturally contented person. What we learn of his character tells us that he may well have been somewhat irascible by nature. One certainly gets the impression, reading his letters, that he did not suffer fools gladly! That may well explain why God sent him a 'thorn ... in the flesh', one that would not be removed, despite a threefold prayer session to that effect! (2 Cor. 12:1-10). God intended to keep him humble!

Similarly, for the psalmist, the road to maturity was an uphill climb that needed the help of the Holy Spirit in order to accomplish it.

A matter of the heart

Secondly, Christian maturity is a disposition of the heart and will. The psalmist pictures a child coming to terms with his new environment. Learning to live without the reassurance of a mother's embrace and a plentiful food supply is a battle that forces a change from within.

It would be easy, for example, to imagine contentment being achieved so long as certain conditions are met:

If only I had a different job, then I would be content...
If only I had a different set of children...
If only I lived in a different house...
If only I had more money...
If only I had different abilities...
If only...

But, the psalmist has learned contentment *with* his circumstances. The environment has not changed, but he has! God changes our hearts and wills.

Perhaps this begs the question whether or not we are engaged in a battle of wills with God, in which we are saying, 'Not thy will, but mine...' There is no peace at the end of that road, only an endless nagging conscience.

Contentment will be tested. It is a rule of the kingdom; God's children are not spared the losses and crosses that accompany life in the footsteps of the Saviour. It is relatively easy to be a Christian when everything is going well: when our marriages are just wonderful, the stock market is bending over backwards to be kind, our job is rewarding and fulfilling. But what if these things were taken away? What would happen then?

That was, of course, Satan's charge concerning Job. He believed that Job would turn and curse God on account of the trials (Job 1:11; 2:5). He was wrong, of course! Job never did curse God, though he got perilously close to it. Job did sin as a result of his trials, something which, in the end, he had to confess to God (Job 42:6). Trials can bring out the best and the worst in us.

In order to learn to swim or to ride a bicycle, at some stage someone has to let go his or her hand. The psalmist is giving expression in this psalm to just that; all the props, the comforts zones, the familiar surroundings, the expectations of each day were changed. He finds himself alone, having to stand for himself. And it is *in* these circumstances and not *beside* them, that he learns contentment.

> For though grace has, in a great measure, rectified the soul and given it a habitual and heavenly temper, yet sin often actually decomposes it again. Thus even a gracious heart is like a musical instrument which, though it is never so exactly tuned, a small matter brings out of tune again. Yes, hang it aside but a little and it will need tuning again before you can play another lesson on it. Even so stands the case with gracious hearts. If they are in frame in one duty, yet they will be dull, dead, and disordered when they come to another. Therefore every duty needs a particular preparation of the heart.
>
> John Flavel, *Keeping the Heart*[1]

The pathway to maturity

Two quite extraordinary statements are found in this psalm that seem puzzling initially, at least.

The first is a statement of the condition of the *heart*. 'My heart is not lifted up', or 'proud', he says (131:1). It is a kind of *Catch 22* statement, isn't it? In saying this, it *sounds* as though a measure of pride is involved! The Hebrew parallelism enables us to catch the sense of what he means:

> O LORD, my heart is not lifted up;
> my eyes are not raised too high.

It is a confession that indicates that he no longer aspires to be something which he isn't. He knows his station; it is to bow before the Sovereign Lord acknowledging God's rule. The psalmist's ambitions have been moulded to conform to those of the Lord's.

A wonderful illustration of this can be seen in the life of King David. David's ambition was to be king of Israel. There was nothing wrong with this ambition; after all, Samuel had anointed him king long before Saul died. What is fascinating about David is not that he aspired to be king, but that he refused to take that aspiration into his own hands and achieve it in such a way that would be contrary to the will of God.

In 1 Samuel 24, when Saul had pursued David to the Desert of En Gedi, David and his men hid themselves in a cave (known locally as the Wildgoats' Rocks!). There came that moment, which Scripture records with all the circumspection that it so often affords in its historical description, when Saul entered the cave, 'to relieve himself' (1 Sam. 24:3). In the darkness, David could easily have slain the king and taken what was destined to be his, but he refused to do so. He did not allow his own ambitions to get the better of him. He would be king, but in God's way, and in God's time. He learned to rein in his heart's ambitions and thus *wait upon the Lord.*

The second aspect of this psalm worthy of attention is the way it suggests that he not only governed his heart, but also controlled the preoccupations of his *mind.* It is just here that the psalm gives expression to a curious statement: 'I do not occupy myself with things too great and too marvellous for me' (131:1). What can he possibly mean? As was stated previously, it sounds like a testimony to the death of all theological reflection! But it can hardly mean that!

What the psalmist means is twofold: he doesn't concern himself with things that are beyond his control or his ability to comprehend.

It is pointless worrying about things we cannot change. And yet, we engage in that pointless activity a great deal! We sow the seeds of what Jesus once called, 'the cares of the world' (Matt. 13:22).

Things happen that are beyond our control to change. We often feel like small grains of sand on the shore facing a relentless incoming tide. The best thing to do, the Christian thing to do, is to hand it all over to the Lord and rest and trust in him.

But more than that, there are things which are beyond our ability to comprehend. This should not surprise us, because it is beyond our ability to comprehend *God*. What we know of God is only a little. We have knowledge only to the extent that he has been pleased to reveal it to us. And what God has revealed is only a tiny fraction of the infinite riches and glory that are his. We could not possibly absorb all that there is to know of God. Over and over, we are forced to cry out, 'Oh, the depth of the riches and wisdom and knowledge of God! How unsearchable are his judgements and how inscrutable his ways!' (Rom. 11:33).

God is incomprehensible. It is not that he cannot be known at all. No, the glory of the gospel is that we *do* come to know him and acknowledge him in the face of Jesus Christ. Jesus Christ 'has made him known' (literally, 'exegetes', John 1:18) to us. Acknowledging this is the pathway to maturity. We cannot fathom the unfathomable.

This does not mean that we do not make any attempt to understand God. We are to ransack the Bible, to read everything that is possible for us to read, to plumb the depths of love divine, and to get to know as much as we can of what God has been pleased to reveal to us. 'Therefore let us leave the elementary doctrine of Christ and go on to maturity...' (Heb. 6:1). We are called to understand as much as we can; but we are to realize, too, that some things, indeed most things, are beyond our comprehension.

This means that we may not understand all that God is doing in our lives; but we are not called upon to understand it; we are called to trust and believe that *he* understands it, and that he has a good and benevolent purpose in mind (see Rom. 8:28).

There is that remarkable moment in the closing chapters of Job where he puts his hand over his mouth (Job 40:4). It is a poignant moment of self-abnegation. He will say no more, not a word! He will be silent before the majesty of God. It is a moment of absolute trust. It is a beautiful moment in which the story finds its resolution — not in understanding, but *in faith*.

It is what this psalm is saying. I will trust and not be afraid. I will not concern myself with things which are above me.

It is, as the puritan Jeremiah Burroughs once put it in a title to a book he wrote, the *Rare Jewel of Christian Contentment*.

For your journal...

1. Write down two areas of your life in which there exists little evidence of Christian maturity.

2. Is *worry* an area of immaturity that you recognize in yourself? Think of one area that concerns you at the moment, and write down two theological truths that inform you that worry is a futile, needless (and *sinful*) exercise!

Psalm 132

A Song of Ascents

1 Remember, O Lord, in David's favour,
    all the hardships he endured,
2 how he swore to the Lord
    and vowed to the Mighty One of Jacob,
3 'I will not enter my house
    or get into my bed,
4 I will not give sleep to my eyes
    or slumber to my eyelids,
5 until I find a place for the Lord,
    a dwelling place for the Mighty One of Jacob.'

6 Behold, we heard of it in Ephrathah;
    we found it in the fields of Jaar.
7 'Let us go to his dwelling place;
    let us worship at his footstool!'

8 Arise, O Lord, and go to your resting-place,
    you and the ark of your might.
9 Let your priests be clothed with righteousness,
    and let your saints shout for joy.
10 For the sake of your servant David,
    do not turn away the face of your anointed one.

¹¹ The LORD swore to David a sure oath
from which he will not turn back:
'One of the sons of your body
I will set on your throne.
¹² If your sons keep my covenant
and my testimonies that I shall teach them,
their sons also for ever
shall sit on your throne.'

¹³ For the LORD has chosen Zion;
he has desired it for his dwelling place:
¹⁴ 'This is my resting-place for ever;
here I will dwell, for I have desired it.
¹⁵ I will abundantly bless her provisions;
I will satisfy her poor with bread.
¹⁶ Her priests I will clothe with salvation,
and her saints will shout for joy.
¹⁷ There I will make a horn to sprout for David;
I have prepared a lamp for my anointed.
¹⁸ His enemies I will clothe with shame,
but on him his crown will shine.'

Day 13

Of covenant mercy I sing...

➤ *Begin by reading Psalm 132.*
➤ *Pray about what you have read.*
➤ *Make notes on what you think God is teaching you.*
➤ *Read the chapter.*
➤ *Answer the questions in the section 'For your journal'.*

Psalm 132

Covenants are keys that unlock the Bible's message. Covenants help us see the unity of God's dealings with his people. They help us focus on the centrality of the gospel. Covenants keep our eyes locked on Jesus Christ.

One of the most beautiful passages in the Old Testament is 2 Samuel 7. It is a passage in which David proposes to build a house (the temple) for the Lord only to learn that God intends to build him one (a faithful lineage that will culminate in the coming of the Saviour). In this passage, God enters into a *covenant* with David. The word 'covenant' does not occur in this passage, but later Scripture is emphatic that what happened here was, in fact, in the form of a covenant (see

2 Sam. 23:5; Ps. 89:3). In particular, this psalm testifies as much! (vv. 11-12).

The pilgrims in Jerusalem, as they stand in the magnificent temple of the Lord, are mindful of its significance for the present and the future. The temple reminded them of past blessings; but it also spoke of blessings that, as yet, were unfulfilled. Hence the prayer of the opening verse, 'Remember, O LORD, in David's favour...' (132:1).

Before the Redeemer came, various foreshadows appeared, displaying one or another aspect of the Redeemer's character and function. David, for example, demonstrated the Messiah's *kingly* office. Jesus would be a king after the pattern of David. The coming king is heir of the covenant made with David.

This psalm is a meditation on that passage in 2 Samuel 7. It focuses on David's reign and its significance in terms of what God was promising to do through it. It is a prayer for God's blessing on David's throne. And as ever with biblical covenants, two parties are involved, making solemn and binding promises (oaths). In this case, it is David who made a vow to the 'Mighty One of Jacob' (132:2), and the Lord who 'swore to David a sure oath' (132:11). The psalm shows a remarkable similarity in both of these sections where David's oath, and then the Lord's oath are considered. Something intensely personal is being done in the covenant of grace: God is drawing near to his people, entering into a relationship with them that will last for ever.

The message on a wreath of flowers from a husband to his departed wife read thus: 'You are eternally in Christ, and for ever in my heart'. It is precisely what the covenant with David promised. Speaking of David's son, Solomon, God would say, 'I will be to him a father, and he shall be to me a son' (2 Sam. 7:14).

The psalm takes into its sweep the progress of redemptive history. God works in time and space. He purposes to save a people for himself by means of a coming Redeemer. As yet, there had been only glimpses of who that Redeemer would be, but there are two focal points in the passage in 2 Samuel. The first is God speaking to David of his death, and Solomon, his son, being raised up to continue to fulfil God's purposes. David's house is linked with Abraham and the promise made to him, 'I will raise up your offspring after you, who shall come from your body, and I will establish his kingdom' (2 Sam. 7:12; compare Gen. 15:15), is part of the ongoing story of redemption that has been unfolding from the first book of the Bible. God is not doing something new; he is fulfilling his ancient promise.

> The whole message of the Bible is shaped around God's coming to us in ... covenant love. The history of God's purposes of salvation centres on the covenants he made with several individuals, and with their families and posterity. We find God making his covenant with Noah, Abraham, Moses, David and finally in Jesus Christ. In each of these covenants we discover who God is, and how fully and completely we can trust him. In fact the message we are meant to hear is this: Down through the centuries God was absolutely faithful to his promises. If he has kept his word all these years, can you not trust him fully and completely too? *He has proved his trustworthiness and faithfulness.*
>
> Sinclair Ferguson, *A Heart for God*[1]

The second focal point of the passage in 2 Samuel 7 comes when God makes it clear to David that there will be an endless Davidic line: 'And your house and your kingdom shall be made sure for ever before me. Your throne shall be established for ever' (2 Sam. 7:16). This theme was to prove powerfully influential in the rest of the Old Testament. It became one of the passages which the faithful of Old Testament times referred to. When life became difficult, when Israel's future seemed in jeopardy, it was to this theme that they turned. Psalm 132 finds the faithful doing just this: praying down the fulfilment of the promises made by God.

David's oath and promise

Two prayers for David mark the beginning of two different sections (vv. 1,10). The first section consists of verses 2-9. In both of these prayers, David is central. The psalm begins, however, with something much more down to earth! There had been a terrible price paid for having a temple in Jerusalem. It had cost the life of one of Israel's sons, Uzzah. The incident in which Uzzah had put out his hand to steady the ark as it stumbled over some rocks, which had caused God to strike him dead, was a painful lesson about reverence and presumption (2 Sam. 6:5-9,12-23). It is this incident, in particular, or at least the history which surrounds it, which is referred to in verse 6. The ark of the covenant had been at Kiriath-Jearim (Jaar of verse 6) for some twenty to thirty years. The Israelites had resorted to using it as a mere talisman against the Philistines. Consequently, God took it from them!

But there were to be hardships for David, too. He would not be allowed to build the temple *himself*. That privilege would be given to Solomon his son. Little wonder, then, that the psalm begins by calling on God to 'remember' all the hardships that David endured! (132:1).

There is a cost to our discipleship, and it is not out of place to ask God to take note of it. The psalm is not expecting God to reward the pains of David, as though the blessings of God are to be earned in some way. Rather, it desires that God take note of the sincerity of David. There was a genuineness to his commitment. If nothing else, David was 'out and out' for the Lord. David swore a vow to take no rest until he should 'find a place for the LORD, a dwelling place for the Mighty One of Jacob' (132:5).

C. H. Spurgeon once wrote, 'Believe me, brethren and sisters, if you never have sleepless hours, if you never have weeping eyes, if your hearts never swell as if they would burst, you need not anticipate that you will be called *zealous*; you do not know the beginning of true *zeal*, for the foundation of Christian *zeal* lies in the heart. The heart must be heavy with grief and yet must beat high with holy ardour; the heart must be vehement in desire, panting continually for God's glory... *Zeal* manifests itself, let me say that it is always seen, where it is genuine, in a vehement love and attachment to the person of the Saviour.'[2]

When the temple was built, Solomon declared at its opening and dedication ceremony that God had no need of a temple, 'Behold, heaven and the highest heaven cannot contain you; how much less this house that I have built!' (1 Kings 8:27). Nevertheless, worshippers in Old Testament times needed a place in which to gather. The tabernacle had all the marks of a temporary dwelling, suitable for that period in which Israel wandered from place to place as a nomadic tribe. But now that Israel was established as a nation, something more substantial and permanent was needed. David gave his desire everything that he had. His oath as recorded here is unrestrained. Nothing will get in the way of achieving his goal for the Lord. Nowhere is this more beautifully seen than in David's resolve to aid Solomon in the accomplishment of this project, even after he himself had been rejected. The Lord's work is too important for personal jealousy and disappointment to disrupt it.

It is an enormous challenge to our commitment to do the Lord's will, even when we face seeming rejection of *our* plans! We are easily bruised. We find ourselves saying, 'If serving the Lord brings me that kind of response, then I'll not serve him. I'll retreat into my little corner, hurt and angry.' It is often our response when God says, 'No!' to some idea of ours that we think is laudable and praiseworthy. There is a lesson for us to learn in this, one that is reflected in the ministry of Jesus and his determination to accomplish his assigned tasks, despite the opposition. He said, 'My food is to do the will of him who sent me and to accomplish his work' (John 4:34).

It is from David's example that the people responded in a similar way by covenanting to take the ark to Jerusalem, its proper resting place. Symbolic as it was of the presence of God, it was not fitting for it to remain where it was.

It is in response to all of this that the psalm now interjects a word of determination from another timeframe: 'Let us go to his dwelling place...' (132:7). As David and his men were determined that God would be worshipped in the right way and in the right location, so others should resolve to do the same. After all, God was there! This was the location where he manifested his presence. It was his 'footstool'. It was the place the sovereign's feet touched the ground, as it were. There should always be a desire to be where God can be found.

True, God is everywhere! That is the message of Psalm 139. But God is especially present at the means of grace, and especially (in Old Testament times) in the tabernacle/temple. This is a truth which carries through into the new covenant also. Jesus could say, for example, in the context of one of the church's most difficult tasks, church discipline, that wherever two or three are gathered together in his name, he is present there (Matt. 18:20). It is that same truth that is reflected in the counsel of the apostle Paul to the Corinthians regarding the use of prophecy. If this is done in an orderly way, and not all at once as was happening in Corinth, unbelievers will be convicted by what they hear and will have cause to say, 'God is really among you' (1 Cor. 14:25).

We ought to have a similar passion for being at the means of grace. We ought to be able to say, as these worshippers were saying, 'Let us go to his dwelling place.' And to what end should this be done? The prayer asks God for two things: that the ministers of the temple be characterized by 'righteousness' and that the saints sing with joy! The former probably has in mind, given the parallel use of 'salvation' in verse 16, that the ministers of the temple speak words that lead to salvation, the salvation which comes through faith alone, and in which an alien righteousness is imputed. Life-giving words and words full of life are what characterize the house of God. Singing the covenant in which sinners are justified in the sight of God is the essence of true worship.

We are called to make a journey from prayer to praise.

The Lord's oath and promise

If the first half of this psalm celebrated David's oath to the Lord (vv. 2-9), the second half celebrates God's oath concerning David (vv. 11-18). The coming king is an heir of the covenant of the Lord. God will set Solomon on the throne of Israel. Despite the fact that David's sons were unimpressive, this was God's promise.

There will always be a Davidic throne! Someone is to sit on David's throne 'for ever' (132:12). Already, we are being introduced to an idea that will mature and grow as the Old Testament progresses. The promise in this psalm, and the one it reflects in 2 Samuel 7, has much more in view than merely the line of succession that continued for 400 years in Jerusalem. There is a seed of another promise here, one which finds its fulfilment in the coming of Jesus as the Saviour of the world. As David's 'greater son', Jesus is the one who now reigns over Zion. Several features of the covenant promise of the coming Saviour now find expression.

God's promise/covenant is irrevocable. His word is utterly trustworthy. It is a 'sure oath from which he will not turn back' (132:11). The covenant of God is inviolable. It cannot be disannulled, for 'all the promises of God find their Yes in him' (2 Cor. 1:20).

> The work which his goodness began,
>   the arm of his strength will complete;
> His promise is yea and amen,
>   and never was forfeited yet.
> Things future nor things that are now,
>   nor all things below or above,
> Can make him his purpose forgo,
>   or sever my soul from his love.
>
>   Augustus Toplady
>   1740-78

The heart of his covenant is God dwelling amongst his people. It is a relationship. It is as verses 13 and 14 (see also v. 8) express it, God's dwelling place, his resting place amongst his people. The ark represented God living and abiding in the midst of the people of God. Ultimately, this is the picture we are given of heaven. In Revelation 7, we have the church triumphant in heaven standing before the throne of God, seeing God in the face of Jesus Christ. There is the most consummate intimacy about it. The Lamb is there, feeding them, leading them to the fountains of living waters. The language of Scripture which describes this relationship is very rich: God is our shepherd who leads us (Ps. 23:1), a soldier who protects us (Josh. 5:13), an encircling army waging war for us (Isa. 63:1-2), a sentry at the door (John 10:3), a broody hen jealously guarding her young (Matt. 23:37).

God provides. The promise of bread, and salvation, in verse 15 is a reminder that God provides for all our needs in the covenant. It is not the promise of enormous wealth (the NIV translation might lead us to think that) but of daily needs and necessities. 'I have been young, and now am old, yet I have not seen the righteous forsaken or his children begging for bread' (Ps. 37:25).

God is triumphant. A sprouting horn (power) and a crown indicate the authority and complete triumph of the covenant mediator (132:17-18). Whatever may have been the glory of the reign of David and of Solomon who followed, it was as nothing compared to the splendour of Christ's reign: 'that in everything he might be preeminent' (Col. 1:18). The psalm which begins with a cross (hardships of David) ends with the crown of King Jesus.

All hail the power of Jesus' name!
Let angels prostrate fall;
Bring forth the royal diadem,
And crown him Lord of all![3]

Edward Perronet
1726-1792

Crown him:

> The one who spoke to wind and sea;
> The one who rebuked legions of demons;
> The one who multiplied loaves and fishes;
> The one who turned water pots into vats of wine;
> The one who defied death and said to Lazarus, 'Come forth!';
> The one who defied his own death and rose from the dead;
> The one who now sits in regal splendour in the session of God's right hand.

You cannot come into contact with Jesus and not be influenced by him in some way.

For your journal...

1. What did the psalmist infer in particular from God's covenant with David?

2. This is a Messianic psalm. What implications does the psalmist draw from this? How does this affect the way you read the Old Testament?

Psalm 133

A Song of Ascents. Of David.

¹ Behold, how good and pleasant it is
    when brothers dwell in unity!
² It is like the precious oil on the head,
    running down on the beard,
on the beard of Aaron,
    running down on the collar of his robes!
³ It is like the dew of Hermon,
    which falls on the mountains of Zion!
For there the LORD has commanded the blessing,
    life for evermore.

Day 14

When oil and water mix

- ➤ *Begin by reading Psalm 133.*
- ➤ *Pray about what you have read.*
- ➤ *Make notes on what you think God is teaching you.*
- ➤ *Read the chapter.*
- ➤ *Answer the questions in the section 'For your journal'.*

Psalm 133

I hate it when the Lord's people quarrel! Don't you?

There are some disagreements which are necessary, of course. When essential truths of the gospel are denied, when practices occur within the church of Jesus Christ that clearly violate scriptural principle, when the honour of Christ is called into question in some way, it is honourable to disagree. It may even be necessary to go on the offensive and engage in battle, even *within the church*!

But, the disagreements that so often mar the church's witness are of a different sort. They are over petty issues of jealousy and pride. Paul could write, for example, to his beloved Philippians exhorting Euodia and Syntyche to be of the same mind (Phil. 4:2). Whatever the precise nature of their squabbling, one can only imagine the shock it must have been when this letter was read out in the church. They are mentioned *by name*! For the apostle, their behaviour was unchristlike, and reprehensible. The fact that it had become public called for a public rebuke!

Psalm 133 is the testimony of a man who is rejoicing in the blessing God bestows upon his people — the blessing of unity. It is one thing to *speak* about unity, and another to '*dwell* in unity' (133:1). Somehow, the psalmist has in mind more than a Bible lesson on Christian unity. He has in mind the actual day-to-day cost of rubbing shoulders with our fellow believers.

Most of us think of Jesus' so-called 'high priestly prayer' in John 17 whenever we think about unity. Jesus prayed that 'all be one' adding by way of a grounding and illustrative metaphor, 'just as you, Father, are in me, and I in you' (John 17:21). The unity of God's people is a matter dear to the heart of Jesus and rooted in the relationship he bears to his Father in heaven. This union, between Father and Son, is one of the impenetrable mysteries of the faith. We could spend eternity contemplating what John means when he says in the prologue to his Gospel, that 'the Word was *with* [Greek, *towards*] God' (John 1:1).

Psalm 133 is a personal reflection on the beauty of unity amongst the people of God. What is stated in the opening verse of the psalm is then illustrated *theologically* (133:2), and *geographically* (133:3). It might be beneficial for us to take this description in reverse order.

Geography lesson

The nature of God's blessing on his worshipping people is described in geographical terms. The psalm mentions two great mountains: Hermon and Zion. In order for us to understand these references we need to engage in some study of historical geography and understand how it is that certain locations became indicative of historical events.

> So long as animosities divide us, and heart-burnings prevail amongst us, we may be brethren no doubt still by common relation to God, but cannot be judged one so long as we present the appearance of a broken and dismembered body. As we are one in God the Father, and in Christ, the union must be ratified amongst us by reciprocal harmony, and fraternal love.
>
> John Calvin, *Commentary on Psalm 133*[1]

Mount Hermon is situated in the northern regions of Israel. A modern traveller, for example, would be able to see its peak from the northern shores of the Sea of Galilee. It is often snow-capped, and its sudden appearance forms one of the most spectacular sights of modern Israel. This writer vividly recalls how, upon first sighting Mount Hermon from the confines of a tour bus, a Presbyterian minister of the Free Church of Scotland burst into a solo rendition of the psalm in Gaelic! Clearly, he was deeply moved by the sight of it, for it spoke to him with great significance.

Apparently, Mount Hermon's cool peaks formed a carpet of condensation on the lower steeps, making the promontory known for its dew.

Mount Zion, on the other hand, is to the south of Hermon, where Jerusalem is built and of far less geographical significance. But it is not the height of Hermon in contrast to Zion that is the point; rather, it is the wet versus dry atmosphere that characterizes both locations. Jerusalem is a dry environment. Within a few miles of the ancient city, a modern traveller can find himself in arid desert. Galilee, on the other hand, is a humid location and modern travellers will notice it immediately.

Do you grasp the point? However uncomfortable the metaphor may sound, the psalmist is saying that worshipping in Jerusalem (Mount Zion) is like waking up in the morning to find that you are covered with dew (as you would be if you slept beneath Mount Hermon's slopes). What can this possibly convey? I have to confess to the thought that waking up all wet isn't my idea of a good time, but that may be missing the point a little. So let us think of it in this way: think of your favourite spot, the place you like to take a vacation. The blessing of God is like being there.

It is like being in another world. You are in Jerusalem, but it is as if you were near the slopes of Hermon. Being with God's people for the celebratory feasts, participating in the worship of God, is like being transported to another place. You lose track of time and place. God's blessings do that! When the dew of heaven falls, it transforms everything it touches. When the dew falls upon the preaching of the Word of God, you are transported into another world. You lose track of your surroundings.

Have you ever imagined yourself walking in the footsteps of some great Bible saint, and wondered what it must have been like to have been in his company? Have you ever walked with Jesus as he went about preaching and performing miracles? In some ways, that is what is being recounted here by this geographical allusion.

But, there is far more to it than an account of some mystical experience. There are Bible truths that highlight for us the significance of these verses. Paul, for example, can speak in Ephesians of Christians being 'seated' with Christ 'in the heavenly places' (Eph. 2:4-7). As well as being in Ephesus, they were sitting with Christ in the heavens! That's a staggering thought, isn't it? In what is almost an offhand remark, Paul introduces his letter to the Philippian church by saying, 'To all the saints in Christ Jesus who are at Philippi' (Phil. 1:1). They are *in Christ* and *at Philippi*!

In an even more astonishing way, Paul can speak of believers as those upon whom the end of the world has dawned (1 Cor. 10:11), and as those who have already begun to taste the powers of the world to come (Heb. 6:5). Isaac Watts can put it this way:

> The men of grace have found,
> Glory begun below;
> Celestial fruits on earthly ground
> From faith and hope may grow.

(Isaac Watts
'Come, we that love the Lord', 1707)

This is what we should pray for and long for in our churches, in the communities of covenant fellowship that we enjoy: that God would be enthroned upon the praises of his people, and that the dew of his heavenly presence would fall in showers of blessing.

Theology lesson

Working backwards through this psalm reveals another metaphor, this time explaining the blessing of God not in terms of local geography, but in terms of Old Testament practice and theology. The blessing of God is like the anointing oil which flowed down over Aaron's beard onto his richly coloured, high-priestly robes (133:2).

The background to this illustration is Exodus 29 where the ritual of the anointing of a high priest is described: 'You shall take the anointing oil and pour it on his head and anoint him' (Exod. 29:7; compare 30:25; Lev. 8:12). However strange this may be to us, the ritual was deeply significant. Aaron was anointed to represent the people of God. He was to execute his ministry *in the place of* others. On his shoulders and his breastplate he carried precious stones on which the names of the families of God's people (the tribes) were inscribed. As he moved into the inner courts of the temple, where no one could gain entry apart from the high priest, he visibly and movingly symbolized the access the people of God had through his ministrations.

In particular, the high priest represented the people of God in three distinct ways: firstly, he officiated at a sacrifice made on their behalf; then secondly, he prayed for their salvation; and thirdly, he came forth from God's presence bringing God's people with him into the holiest place of all, to meet with God in the glory of his presence. If you were to ask someone, 'Where does the blessing of God come from?', the answer would be, 'It comes from the high priest. He got it for me. He brought it to me and shared it with all God's people.'

Two things seem to warrant some comment.

Firstly, there is the extravagance of the anointing. The quantity of oil and perfume used meant that it ran down the high priest's face and beard and onto his clothes. It was deeply symbolic of the blessings of God that came through the high priests, for they are never desultory. *'There is wideness to God's mercy,'* we sing, and the thought is the same here. God intends to bless his people richly, by richly blessing his servant the high priest.

But secondly, it is the high priest, and he alone, who is the focus of attention. No blessings come apart from him. God blesses through *him*. And we are meant to catch the New Testament fulfilment of this; for we, too, have a High Priest, Jesus Christ. The book of Hebrews, for example, draws attention to him in this office. At one telling moment, the writer exhorts his readers in this way: 'Therefore, holy brothers, you who share in a heavenly calling, consider Jesus, the apostle and high priest of our confession' (Heb. 3:1). In some ways, that is what this psalm is doing: urging us to look to Jesus Christ in his glorious office as High Priest.

Have you felt the blessings of God come flooding into your soul as you have worshipped amongst the people of God recently? Why is that so? What accounts for it? It is that Jesus has gone as our representative, as our great High Priest, into the inner sanctuary of the temple, taking the blood of the everlasting covenant with him (Heb. 8 - 9). He has obtained redemption for us. He has expiated our sins, propitiated God's wrath, redeemed us from the curse, and satisfied God's law, by substituting himself.

Consider Jesus!

No blessing comes apart from him. Perhaps this explains why we sometimes miss the blessing — we take our eyes off Jesus. We do not make him central in our lives. We do not meditate upon his glory.

It is because the Father loved him so that we can begin to understand what might have been the cost of these blessings.

All our blessings come in Jesus Christ: the blessings of eternal election, of free justification, of adoption and forgiveness, of perseverance, and of final glorification. Each one comes by virtue of his completed work for us.

Every mark of a true church is by virtue of our High Priest.

- It is the voice of Jesus Christ we hear in the faithful preaching of God's Word (John 10:4).
- It is the voice of Jesus Christ who leads the singing on Sunday mornings and evenings (Heb. 2:12). He sings along with us, sharing our hymn books!
- It is Jesus Christ who reveals himself, as in a mirror, in the celebration of the sacraments (1 Cor. 10:16).
- It is Jesus Christ who is present in the church, distributing gifts (Eph. 4:7) and, perhaps surprisingly, in the discipline of an offending brother (1 Cor. 5:3-5).
- 'That which we have seen and heard we proclaim also to you, so that you too may have fellowship with us; and indeed our fellowship is with the Father and with his Son Jesus Christ' (1 John 1:3).

But there is one very distinct way in which the high-priestly ministry of Christ is meant to comfort us. The writer to the Hebrews makes a telling comment by alluding to the fact that Jesus occupied the office of the High Priest in weakness. In this way, he is able to sympathize with us in our weakness (Heb. 4:14-16). In the only direct reference to Psalm 133 in the New Testament, it is to this issue that it refers. Writing to the Corinthians, Paul could say, 'For as we share abundantly in Christ's sufferings, so through Christ we share abundantly in comfort too' (2 Cor. 1:5). Like the oil which flowed over Aaron's head and down his robes, so the sufferings and comfort of Christ flow down to us.

Focusing on Jesus will remind us of what to expect in our lives: suffering *and* comfort. Not one without the other. Never!

Ecclesiastical lesson

A third feature of this psalm emerges, and it is expressed in the opening verse. The psalmist is reflecting on the blessings, and when God's blessings come, the people of God live together in gracious unity. Unity is (objectively) *good*, and (subjectively) *pleasant*. But there is a subtle twist that reminds us that this unity is not always manifested as it should be. It is the Lord who commands the blessing (133:3), *and not us*; but, it is we who do the living, the dwelling together, *and not the Lord* (133:1).

Whenever we experience the Lord's blessing in worship, we ought to greet one another as the Lord's people. Covenant blessings ought to inspire covenant recognition. In New Testament times, it was a 'holy kiss' (1 Thess. 5:26). Whatever form that may now take, we are commended to demonstrate that unity which is the result of our receiving his blessing.

It is as though the Lord is saying to his assembled congregations, 'Blessing, blessing, blessing … this is what I give to you.' And when you receive it — foretastes of his glory — can you then harm the unity of God's people by some unkind word, some selfish motive, some mean-spirited gesture?

The psalm actually puts it the other way around. Where unity is seen to exist, it is *there* 'the LORD has commanded the blessing' (133:3).

> Command Thy blessing from above,
> O God, on all assembled here;
> Behold us with a Father's love,
> While we look up with filial fear.

Command Thy blessing in this hour,
Spirit of truth, and fill the place
With humbling and exalting power,
With quickening and confirming grace.

O Thou, our Maker, Saviour, Guide,
One true eternal God confessed,
May nought in life or death divide
Thy saints in Thy communion blest.

With Thee and these for ever bound,
May all who here in prayer unite,
With harps and songs Thy throne surround,
Rest in Thy love, and reign in light.

James Montgomery
1771-1854

For your journal...

1. Ask yourself today, 'Do I encourage true unity or disunity in God's church?' Are there things that you can change in order to ensure that you encourage unity?

2. Write down four things that are troubling the church you belong to, and pray about each one specifically.

Psalm 134

A Song of Ascents

1 Come, bless the LORD, all you servants of the LORD,
   who stand by night in the house of the LORD!
2 Lift up your hands to the holy place
   and bless the LORD!

3 May the LORD bless you from Zion,
   he who made heaven and earth!

Day 15

The benediction

> ➤ *Begin by reading Psalm 134.*
> ➤ *Pray about what you have read.*
> ➤ *Make notes on what you think God is teaching you.*
> ➤ *Read the chapter.*
> ➤ *Answer the questions in the section 'For your journal'.*

Psalm 134

There is something appropriately climactic about this final psalm in the series known as the Psalms of Ascent. It is a call to worship *and* a benediction! In a way, it is an 'Amen' on all that has gone before in the fifteen Psalms of Ascent.

In the church where I serve, for example, this psalm is recited frequently on Sunday evenings as a call to worship.

In the history of worship, the Reformers (who were deliberately looking back to the Patristic roots of worship) taught that formal worship ought to be contained within two 'bookends' that clearly set it apart from anything else that we do. These two 'bookends' were *The call to worship* at the very beginning and *The benediction* at the close. One of

the immediate effects of this is obvious. It establishes a point
after we have gathered when all conversation and personal
fellowship gives way to the worship of Almighty God. Try
announcing a hymn when everybody is still talking and it will
become obvious how difficult it is to establish some decorum
and reverence. *The call to worship* announces that it is time to
cease all idle chatter and concentrate on the living God!

Psalm 134 is also a 'blessing': 'May the LORD bless you
from Zion.' It would therefore be equally fitting as a benediction. Martin Luther, for example, emphasized the importance of the benediction at the *close* of worship. He suggested
that it should be the Aaronic benediction from Numbers
6:24-26:

> The LORD bless you and keep you;
> the LORD make his face to shine upon you and be gracious
>   to you;
> the LORD lift up his countenance upon you and give you
>   peace.

You will remember that, following the resurrection, after
Jesus had met with the disciples by the Sea of Galilee he led
them towards the region of Bethany where, 'lifting up his
hands he blessed them' (Luke 24:50). It was while he was doing
this that he ascended up into heaven (24:51). Benedictions are
a reminder of Jesus' blessing. It sets worship in a covenant
context; the blessings of God are being bestowed upon his
worshipping people.

One of the things that we need to notice about the form
of words used in the Aaronic benediction, or the many others
that have been highlighted in Scripture (e.g. the Apostolic
benediction of 2 Corinthians 13:14, including the closing
verse of this psalm), is that it is *a blessing* and not *a prayer*.

That is why many Christians keep their eyes open during the benediction. The minister is pronouncing the blessing of God upon his people, rather than praying to God for it.

The concept of the covenant is portrayed beautifully in this psalm. The Lord's people are blessing God and God is blessing them. It isn't obvious in the New International Version, but the word 'Praise' in verse 1 is exactly the same word as 'bless' in verse 3. We *bless* the Lord, and the Lord *blesses* us! There is nothing more wonderful than that! It is that for which we were created. It is that for which we were redeemed.

The psalm falls into two segments: the initial call to praise/bless (vv. 1-2), followed by the benediction of the Lord (v. 3).

Praise the Lord!

The command to bless or praise the Lord is given, not to all the worshippers present, but to a specific group of worshippers: 'servants of the LORD'. Who are they? They are said to serve (literally, 'stand') by night in the house of the LORD. These are the Levitical priests who served in the temple, performing detailed ministrations as directed by the cultic legislation of the Old Testament. The fact that they were doing this 'by night' suggests that this may well have been the all-night vigil kept during the festival of the Passover (see Exod. 12:42). In 1 Chronicles 9 we read of certain Levites who lodged in the temple. It was their task to open and shut the massive gates, keep the vessels clean, take charge of the supplies of flour and wine, and attend to the ovens which baked the shewbread; some were even employed as night porters and guards to apprehend vagrants. Perhaps the psalmist has in mind these people on night-duty.

Some have suggested that the two sections of the psalm, verses 1-2 and verse 3, are the responsive calls of night-shift workers to each other as one ends and another begins his temple work shift.

Perhaps the worshipper was present in the outer courts of the temple and now summons the priests to praise the Lord. It was part of their work 'to carry the ark of the covenant of the LORD to stand before the LORD to minister to him and to bless in his name' (Deut. 10:8).

But what exactly are they being called upon to do? What does it mean to *bless* the Lord? Sometimes, it simply means 'to praise'. It is certainly appropriate for priests, as well as every other believer, to praise the Lord. But this doesn't do full justice to the word used here. *Blessing* carries with it a host of associations that 'praise' does not.

The word used is well known to us because of Jeremiah's amanuensis, Baruch. His name means either that he was one who was the recipient of blessing, or more probably, that he was the source of blessing (particularly to his parents who named him *Baruch*). The word occurs in its many forms over 400 times in the Old Testament, and is amongst one of the most common words to be found in the pages of Scripture. On a few occasions, it is translated as 'kneel' and some have argued that blessing and kneeling are strongly related. If the idea of physical kneeling isn't to be taken too strongly (and it probably isn't), the connotations of reverence and humility certainly are.

> Bless the LORD, O my soul,
>   and all that is within me,
>   bless his holy name!
>   (Ps. 103:1, 2, 20, 21, 22 [twice]).

O Jesus, my Saviour, thy blessed humility! Impress it on
my heart, make me most sensible of thy infinite dignity,
and of my own vileness, that I may hate myself as a thing
of naught, and be willing to be despised, and trodden
upon by all, as the vilest mire of the streets, that I may still
retain these words, 'I am nothing, I have nothing, I can do
nothing, and I desire nothing but one.'

Robert Leighton, 'Rules and Instructions for a Holy Life'[1]

Blessing God involves reviewing his excellencies, and
responding to them accordingly, in reverent worship. (When
God blesses us, he reviews our needs and responds to them,
as we shall see.) In Psalm 103, a well-known phrase reminds
us that we are to 'forget not all his benefits' (Ps. 103:2). The
psalm goes on to enumerate the reasons for blessing him,
which include forgiveness, healing, preservation, and the idea
that 'every spiritual blessing' is ours through his grace.

The worship of God, which blessing him involves, is
primarily theological: it is a response to what we know of God
and his ways. We bless him because he blesses us; as Psalm
133 has already reminded us, 'the LORD has commanded the
blessing' (Ps. 133:3). Just as marriages grow sour through
lack of affectional response, so our relationship with God
gets thrown out of kilter whenever we do not bless him for
all he has done for us. Just as worship involves extolling
God's *worth*-ship, so blessing God involves commending his
wonderful being.

By way of implication, this concluding psalm of the series
has some valuable things to tell us about worship.

Firstly, worship consists largely in thanksgiving. According
to Shakespeare, in his play, *As You Like It*, unthankfulness is
one of cruellest expressions of human selfishness.

Blow, blow, thou winter wind,
Thou art not so unkind
    As man's ingratitude:
Thy tooth is not so keen,
Because thou art not seen,
    Although thy breath be rude.

We can never praise God enough, and those who lead
in the worship of God, whose task it is to superintend the
administrations of the temple, must ensure that the Lord is
duly praised.

Praise, my soul, the King of heaven,
To His feet Thy tribute bring;
Ransomed, healed, restored, forgiven,
Who like Thee His praise should sing?
Praise Him! Praise Him!
Praise the everlasting King.

                                        Henry Francis Lyte
                                        1793-1847

Secondly, the worship of the Levitical priests was to
continue long after the worshippers present had gone home.
It would be interesting to think that these worshippers who
now call upon the Levites to bless the Lord, and who are
embarking on their journey back to Meshech and Kedar (Ps.
120:5), need that praise to continue as they journey home.
Travelling at night would have been much cooler for them,
and it would be consistent to imagine them gathering 'one last
time' in the temple precincts before returning home. 'Keep
doing your work as we journey home!' they might be saying.

   If this is indeed what is happening here, then it would be
fitting to see a New Testament fulfilment of this picture. We

have a great High Priest whose intercessions continually bring us blessings from the right hand of God (see Heb. 4:14-15; 5:1; 6:20; 7:26). As we, too, make our journey home, we are in need of his intercessions and offerings on our behalf. It is Jesus who continually secures for us the blessings of the covenant of grace.

Thirdly, there is a lesson here about posture and worship. 'Lift up your hands to the holy place' (134:3) could easily be taken as an argument in favour of this practice whenever worship is offered to God. The practice seemed to have been done in New Testament times. Paul can instruct: 'I desire then that in every place the men should pray, lifting holy hands...' (1 Tim. 2:8). Calvin, speaking of this passage, says that Paul 'uses the outward sign for the inward reality, for our hands indicate a pure heart'. Actually, the Scriptures use a variety of postures and gestures in prayer, including standing and kneeling (which resembled more of a prostration than we tend to imagine). Thus, the Levites summoned the people to 'stand up and bless the LORD your God from everlasting to everlasting' (Neh. 9:5). Whilst standing, it was common either to lift hands or spread them before the Lord (Ps. 28:2; Lam. 3:41; compare Exod. 9:29; 17:11-12; 1 Kings 8:22; Neh. 8:6; Pss 63:4; 143:6). The eyes could either be lifted up in expectation (e.g. Pss 25:15; 121:1; 123:1-2) or cast down in penitence (Luke 18:13). Slouching is *not* the right posture for worship!

The Lord bless you!

As we have already noted, the response of the Levites to their being called to bless the Lord is to pronounce the Lord's blessing upon the people. What an encouragement that would have been, and how fitting, for those about to embark on their journey home! They would go with the blessing of God upon them.

It is customary to end a service of worship with a benediction, pronounced by a minister of the Word of God. The rite has been carefully guarded as a function of an ordained minister of the Word alone. It is customary still, for example, at the ordination service of a minister, following his ordination, to conduct him to the pulpit and ask him to pronounce the benediction. Whilst all Christians are priests in the new covenant, not all Christians are ministers of the Word and the sacraments.

But what does it mean to pronounce a blessing upon the congregation of God's people? To pronounce:

'The grace of the Lord Jesus Christ and the love of God and the fellowship of the Holy Spirit be with you all'

(2 Cor. 13:14)

or,

'Now may the God of peace who brought again from the dead our Lord Jesus, the great shepherd of the sheep, by the blood of the eternal covenant, equip you with everything good that you may do his will, working in us that which is pleasing in his sight, through Jesus Christ, to whom be glory for ever and ever. Amen'

(Heb. 13:20-21)

or even the simpler form,

'The grace of our Lord Jesus Christ be with you'

(1 Thess. 5:28)

is to utter words of the most solemn nature imaginable. In these New Testament forms, *bless* is equivalent to *grace*. It is a reminder that in 'counting our blessings', each one is a bestowal that has its origin in the grace of God.

Though blessing is a broad term, its meaning, particularly in the Old Testament, is quite specific. God's blessing includes children, property, land, good health, and particularly his presence (Gen. 17:16; 22:17 following; Lev. 26:3-13; Deut. 28:2-14). We have already seen an allusion to the Aaronic benediction of Numbers 6 in Psalm 121, where the blessing alluded to is that 'the LORD will keep you from all evil; he will keep your life... your going out and your coming in from this time forth and for evermore' (Ps. 121:7-8). Psalm 67 is another psalm which echoes this benediction, and there the blessing includes the fact that the 'earth has yielded its increase' (Ps. 67:6).

It is 'from Zion' that the blessing of God comes (134:3). And in new covenant terms, it is from the heavenly Jerusalem that all mercies descend (Heb. 12:22-24). But the focus is not entirely heavenward. It is God 'who made heaven and earth' who now blesses. Its deliberate echoes of Genesis 1 are a reminder of God's power. He who blesses has *power* to bless! His blessing is no light thing, but a force to be reckoned with.

But more than that, the blessing obviously has the overtones of a covenant. By this pronouncement, we are reckoned amongst the spiritual lineage of Abraham and Isaac and Jacob. We are amongst the people of God upon whom God's distinct-ive love continues to be poured, no matter what else may be true. It is that thought that enables these worshippers to go home in peace. The love of God will follow them, until they meet again in Jerusalem. And it will follow every child of God — for ever.

Great is Thy Faithfulness, O God my Father,
There is no shadow of turning with Thee;
Thou changest not, Thy compassions they fail not;
As Thou hast been Thou for ever wilt be.

Great is Thy faithfulness! Great is Thy faithfulness!
Morning by morning new mercies I see!
All I have needed Thy hand hath provided —
Great is Thy faithfulness, Lord unto me!

Summer and winter, and springtime and harvest,
Sun, moon and stars in their courses above,
Join with all nature in manifold witness
To Thy great faithfulness, mercy and love.

Pardon for sin and a peace that endureth,
Thine own dear presence to cheer and to guide,
Strength for today and bright hope for tomorrow,
Blessings all mine, with ten thousand beside!

Thomas O. Chisolm
1866-1960

That says it all, I think, except for this: that the verb in verse
3 is singular, whereas in verses 1 and 2 it is plural. What does
that mean? It may mean simply this: that the blessing of God
finds you wherever you are, whoever you are.

That's a thought worth pondering for a lifetime!

For your journal...

1. As you come to the end of this book, write down as many things you can think of which confirm that you have made progress in the discipline of spiritual devotions.

2. Write down plans which state the ways in which you intend to continue this discipline for the next few months.

Notes

Preface
1. Alec Motyer, *Journey: Psalms for Pilgrim People* (Nottingham, England: IVP, 2010). Motyer suggests a triadic compilation which is fascinating.

Introduction
1. *Confessions*, 1:1.
2. Found in his major work *de Spiritualibus Ascensionibus* ('on spiritual ascents').
3. The Banner of Truth, 1978, p.9.
4. Commentary on 1 Peter 1:11.
5. John Calvin, *Institutes,*I.xi.8.
6. Eugene H. Peterson, *A Long Obedience in the Same Direction*, IVP, USA, 2000 (1980).
7. Donald S. Whitney, *Spiritual Disciplines for the Christian Life*, Scripture Press, 1991, p.195. Whitney writes a marvellous chapter in this book on the benefits of journaling as *a discipline*.

Day 1: A godly man in an ungodly world
1. *Commentary on The Book of Psalms*, Vol. 2, Baker Book House, 1981, p.207.

2. J. I. Packer, foreword to Leyland Ryken's *Worldly Saints: The Puritans as They Really Were*, Academie Books, 1986, p.xi.
3. The Banner of Truth, 1968, p.153.
4. The hymn begins: 'Stand up, stand up for Jesus', by George Duffield, Jr, (1858).
5. Cited by John Piper, *Desiring God*, IVP, 1989, p.29.
6. The closing lines of Oswald Allen's hymn, written in 1861: 'Today Thy Mercy calls me to wash away my sin'.

Day 2: Needing help

1. It is important to realize that this is God's *proper* name, rather than a title, and hence 'LORD' rather than 'the LORD' is the better way of describing the intent of the Old Testament at this point. He is 'LORD' rather than 'He is *the* LORD.'
2. Presbyterian and Reformed Publishing, 2000, pp.193-94.

Day 3: Jerusalem

1. S. M. Houghton, 'From Amman to Jerusalem' in *The Banner of Truth* 49 (July/August 1967), p.12.
2. 1862-64 reprint. The Banner of Truth, 1973, Vol. 1, p.192.

Day 4: Eyes right

1. *The Shorter Catechism*, Answer 98.
2. Christian Focus Publications, 1999, pp.109-10.

Day 5: If God be for us...

1. John Calvin, *The Institutes of the Christian Religion*, I.xvii.1.
2. New York, Harcourt Brace Jovanovich, 1964, p.113.
3. John Calvin, *Institutes* II.xvi.6.

Day 6: Surrounded

1. John Calvin, *Psalms*, Baker Book House, 1981 reprint, 1571, xxxvii.
2. Ed. John T. McNeill, trans. Ford Lewis Battles, 2 Vols, The Westminster Press, 1975, 1:712 (III. ix.1).
3. John Bunyan, *Prayer*, The Banner of Truth, 1965 reprint, 1662, p.13.

Day 7: Holy tears and holy laughter

1. 163, Job 38:31. Reading for the evening of 21 March, MacDonald Publishing Co., 1973.

Day 8: Built to last

1. Fanny Crosby's hymn, 'All the way my Saviour leads me', was written in 1875.
2. Eagle Publishing, 1995, p.92.

Day 9: Bless this house

1. John Newton's hymn: 'Glorious things of thee are spoken', 1779.

Day 10: The Lord is righteous

1. 'It is monstrously simple-minded to read the cursings in the Psalms with no feeling except one of horror at the uncharity of the poets. They are indeed devilish.' C. S. Lewis, *Reflections on the Psalms,* Collins/Fontana Books, 1957, p.27.
2. Macmillan Publishing Co. Inc., 1950, p.133.
3. C. H. Spurgeon, *Treasury of David*, 7:60.

Day 11: Out of the depths

1. J. C. Ryle, *Holiness*, James Clark & Co., 1956, p.1. This book is now available from EP Books.
2. The Banner of Truth, 1989, p.37.

Day 12: A weaned soul
1. *Soli Deo Gloria*, 1998, p.6.

Day 13: Of covenant mercy I sing...
1. The Banner of Truth, 1987, p.37.
2. C. H. Spurgeon, *Spurgeon's Expository Encyclopedia*, Vol. 15, p.421.
3. Edward Perronet's hymn, 'All Hail the Power of Jesus' name', 1779.

Day 14: When oil and water mix
1. *Commentary on the book of Psalms*, trans. Rev. James Anderson, Baker Book House, 1981, p.164.

Day 15: The benediction
1. Henry Scougal, *The life of God in the Soul of Man*, Christian Heritage Series, Christian Focus Publications, 1996, pp.139-59. This prayer comes at section III:14.

Notes...

Notes...

Notes...